MAURICE RICKARDS

THE PUBLIC NOTICE

AN ILLUSTRATED HISTORY

Clarkson N. Potter, Inc./Publisher NEW YORK

DISTRIBUTED BY CROWN PUBLISHERS, INC.

Inquiries should be addressed to Clarkson N. Potter, Inc.,
419 Park Avenue South, New York, N.Y. 10016.
Library of Congress Catalog Card Number: 73–77336

SBN : 0–517–504766

Printed in Great Britain

First American edition published in 1973
by Clarkson N. Potter, Inc.

Designed by Maurice Rickards

AUTHOR'S NOTE

This collection could not have been brought together without the help of a large number of institutions and private individuals. Their contributions, in the form of information concerning notices and notice-lore, or as photographs and reproductions of actual examples, have come from far and wide. Names of contributors and informants are listed on page 126.

Special thanks are due to a number of these. I am particularly indebted to the archivists of the Dorset County Museum for access to the Shipp Collection of printed broadsides and ephemera, and to the curator of the Museum of English Rural Life, Reading, for similar help with the collection of the printed work of the Soulbys of Ulverston.

The Museum of British Transport has also provided invaluable help; so have the Tower Hamlets Libraries Committee, the New York Public Library, the London Museum, the British Museum, the New York Historical Society, the St Bride Printing Library, the National Library of Ireland, the Guildhall Library, the Imperial War Museum and many others.

Among the private individuals who have given special help, particular thanks are due to Mrs Katherine Newell of Newcastle-upon-Tyne, whose holiday snapshot drew attention to the imperishable declaration of the County of Middlesex (illustration 248), and to Mr Peter Scott of Sydney, whose classic trespass item appears as illustration 243.

The provenance of each illustrated item is indicated in an individual credit line; where the contribution has been merely textual, however, I regret that it has not been possible to link the name of the informant with the specific item. I trust that the contributor will bear with me in this failure of detail.

A word as to times and places: although the majority of notices – particularly the printed ones – normally include the date and place of publication within their own text, these details are here noted beneath the illustrations regardless of whether or not they appear in the picture. In the case of wood, metal and other notices, two dates may be given: the first refers to the time of the notice's first appearance; the second, in square brackets, shows when it was photographed. (The Dorset bridge notice – illustration No 2 – may thus be seen to have remained on active service for over 140 years.) The presence of a second date indicates that the notice was still *in situ* when the photograph was taken; where no second date is given for a wood or metal specimen, the item has been photographed in retirement, in a museum or private collection. Modern items, in which the illustration bears only one date, were photographed at about the time of their appearance.

The majority of the notices in the collection are self-explanatory (it is in the nature of things that the public notice speaks for itself) but the reader may find the text helpful in elucidating the background to certain items. Illustrations are referred to throughout the text by numbers in square brackets. These relate to picture numbers, not to pages.

If a number of the illustrations are of less than first-class quality, it will be borne in mind that many are from old and ailing originals; some have only just managed to survive at all. (Apart from specimens in museums, the public notice has till now tended to be an underprivileged candidate for conservation.) In many cases the specimen has been photographed in bad light with a hand-held holiday camera; the reader will recognize the symptoms.

What matters, one may venture to hope, is not so much that they have been recorded ill or well, but that they have been recorded at all.

MAURICE RICKARDS
November 1972

THE PUBLIC NOTICE

THE PRINTED PUBLIC ANNOUNCEMENT is essentially an instrument of public control. Historically, it represents an extension of the power of the ruler – authority mass-produced. In large measure it has retained this role to the present day. Its history is the history of organized society.

It is a matter of some surprise that its influence on affairs should have been so profound. Even into our own times, it has exerted forces bordering almost on the magical.

Though often imperfectly obeyed, and more often apparently ignored, the notice nonetheless operates as a distinguishable social force; its strength is seen, if in nothing else, in the attraction it holds as a subject for defacement. It has many of the attributes of the totem pole; you may venerate it, you may seek its destruction, but it is very hard to ignore it.

Much of the magic of the notice may be traced to the power of the written word – more particularly, of the printed word. Even today, in a sceptical and wayward world, where established power hangs on uncertainly and obedience is by no means a built-in reflex, the printed word still carries weight.

In business, in diplomacy, in public life, its mystique prevails. At every level the document wins where the spoken word is scarcely deemed to exist. 'Please write in' is a standard response to a verbal approach in industry or commerce. The expression, 'I saw it in black and white', though less widely used today than once, is still heard as an assurance of probity. The health of the written word, notwithstanding the effects of radio and television, continues moderately good.

For an explanation of its power the social historian looks to its history. In earliest times the art of writing was the private skill of a powerful minority. Whether priesthood or lay aristocracy, the ruling class alone had leisure and learning enough to master it. It was logical for the ordinary man to equate the skill with the power that went with it.

Writing, it appeared, was a function of command – even of divine command. It was not merely an instrument; it was much more than that: it was command itself – the invisible made visible. In the natural order of things, he who wrote was *ipso facto* he who made

the rules. The principle was transparently clear.

It is here, at the very heart of the phenomenon of writing, that the study of the printed notice begins. For many, the notice is an item of printed ephemera, a suitable subject for connoisseurs and collectors of bygones. But the notice is also an expression of deep-seated social forces; in conception, form and content it expresses crucial areas of the human condition. Its origins are close to the origins of law,

FITZROY COLLECTION

Persons stealing from or committing wilful damage to this kiosk render themselves liable to imprisonment

DORSET
ANY PERSON WILFULLY INJURING ANY PART OF THIS COUNTY BRIDGE WILL BE GUILTY OF FELONY AND UPON CONVICTION LIABLE TO BE TRANSPORTED FOR LIFE BY THE COURT
7&8 GEO 4 C30 S 13   T FOOKS

1 London 1966   **2** Dorset *c* 1829 [1970]

order, government and the hierarchy of power. Its basic attitudes, whatever its epoch, whatever its form [1, 2],* are constant.

For the exercise of power, two forms of communication are needed. One is channelled inwards, towards the centre of power; the other is outward, from the governor to the governed. Without both channels, power cannot properly be said to exist. 'Intelligence', received from the field, formulates policy; policy is transmitted to the field in the form of commands. The cycle is primordial.

The earliest commands – edicts, instructions, orders – were spoken, and sometimes literally shouted. Xerxes, King of Persia, set up 'shouting chains' of soldiers to transmit messages throughout the kingdom. He could convey an order to any point in the country in twenty-four hours. Other rulers merely spoke their messages to athletes, who ran with them as directed – sometimes, as with Pheidippides after the battle of Marathon, dropping dead with exhaustion on delivery.

Figures in brackets refer to illustrations.

7

The development of writing allowed longer and more detailed orders to be transmitted. These ranged from the *ad hoc* command of the moment to long-term rules and regulations of Law and Order. They served both in the military and civil spheres (often there was no very clear distinction between the two) and, because literacy was slow to spread, they relied for final delivery on an elite of official 'readers'.

Thus it was that for centuries the public crier (or Town Major, or Constable, or whatever he was called), receiving a written command from central government, proceeded to read it aloud before posting it up.

In this way, too, the document came to be seen as a tangible contact with the very will and person of the ruler himself. Summoned by drum or trumpet to the market-place, the people saw the actual document unrolled – direct, presumably, from the actual hand of majesty – and heard its oracular pronouncement. With the reading done, and the text duly posted, they gathered round to see the document. It was almost as though the monarch himself had come among them.

They were not to know, as technology overtook them, that the marks upon the paper had been made by machine instead of man. Early printers were at pains to counter resistance to their craft, and took trouble to make their characters as much like hand-written ones as possible. To the untutored eye, if not to that of the *literato*, the effect was indistinguishable from the real thing.

It was in situations like these, with the order or proclamation evolving from a mode of transmission to an exhibit in its own right, that the notice developed as a social instrument. In its appearance among ordinary people it combined a sense of occasion, a sense of the charisma of kings and of the mystery of the written word.

Above all – and in many cases literally – its word was law; the posting of a notice or proclamation was often in itself an act of government. In a context of virtually continual alarm and unrest there was no device so handy and so often utilized:

> ... it was a universal instrument of rule. It declared war, raised the price of bread, threatened to shoot hostages, exaggerated victories, justified retreats, ordered rejoicings, stamped out mutinies and deeply mourned dead rulers while simultaneously welcoming their replacements.*

The Notice was *The Law*. New ordinances, chapter, section and article, were posted up as soon as they were passed. Often their effects were matters

* The Rise and Fall of the Poster (*David & Charles*).

of life and death. It is not surprising that through the generations, ordinary people came to view the notice with a special awe.

Nor is it surprising that Authority exploited it so thoroughly. Nor that a special notice-vocabulary evolved. Aware of its impact on the rank and file, and mindful of its exalted station, the Notice expressed itself in the resounding language of the throne room. Beginning often with 'Whereas' – a lead-in which was to become ingrained in the syntax of all notice-makers – and rolling through lengthy preambular cadences before coming to the point, the composition made full use of royal plurals, honorifics, imperial signatures and other such devices.

Chief among the characteristics of the proclamatory notice is its fulsome sense of its own justification. It presents a cast-iron case. The proclaimant establishes his status, qualifications, antecedents, etc. He sketches the historical background, spells out his reasons for the present declaration, and sometimes even regales the reader with a homilly on the duties and responsibilities of government.

The convention is not confined to the English-speaking world. In October 1789, three months after the storming of the Bastille, but with Louis XVI still retained as the nation's head, the National Assembly put out a Declaration. Entitled *Déclaration du Roi*, the announcement reported a twelve-article decree for the establishing of martial law. The decree effectively constituted a French 'Riot Act'. In its preamble it provided a potted summary of the rationale of Law and Order:

> The National Assembly, considering that Liberty strengthens empires, but that Licence destroys them; that far from conferring the right to do everything, liberty exists only through obedience to laws; that although during times of tranquility this obedience is adequately assured by the ordinary public authority, there may arise difficult periods where the people, stirred up by often criminal influences, become the instrument of intrigues of which they are ignorant; that these times of crisis momentarily require extraordinary measures for the maintenance of the public peace and the preservation of the rights of all, has decreed and decrees the present Martial Law ...

Three years later, on 10 August 1792, in a further invocation of calm and respectability, a proclamation by the National Assembly declared that although the king had now been formally relieved of his duties, his signature would none the less still be appearing on decrees, regardless of whether or not they had been sanctioned by him. All decrees, declared before or after his suspension of power, would carry his name as usual. 'The formula will continue to be employed', the proclamation said.

The proclamation writer grasps at any legal-sounding verbal straw. In 1861, uncertain of the weight of their unsupported names at the foot of their appeal for recruits to the Virginia Volunteers [124], the signatories inserted the foot-line, *Done by Authority*. In 1868, when the Vigilance Committee of Southern Indiana put out its warning to its enemies ('short shrift and a hempen collar') [33], it felt constrained to establish its credentials with a quotation from Cicero: *Salus populi suprema lex.**

A similar respect for the decencies, this time purely administrative, appears in a Workers' Soviet proclamation in Munich in 1919. Here the population is warned that counter-revolutionary acts of any kind will be punished by shooting. In a neat inversion of the normal order of things, the notice invokes the authority of decrees still to be disclosed; it refers the reader to 'ordinances concerning the State of Siege, to be published later'.

Perhaps the most impressive of all examples of mock-legality is that of the celebration call put out on the occasion of the surrender of General Lee to General Grant in 1865 [171]. This instructs all businesses to close at 2 o'clock, and the people 'to be on hand to sing and rejoice'. It closes with the footline *By Order of the People*.

The 'public notice' idiom

Spurious or not, the note of legal standing dies hard. Even in its obviously unofficial forms, where the notice-giver is a simple private citizen, phraseology aspires to legalese. Most frequent – and least meaningful – of all such phrases is the ubiquitous *By Order*. Like the equally meaningless *As of and from 1 April*, the expression has acquired overtones of respectability.

It is fitting that the notice, as champion of law and order (and as defender not only of the faith but of private property and public decency) should adopt a sober tone. Its general level, whether offering money for the capture of a runaway slave or warning of the consequences of placing obstacles on the railway line, is one of grim self-righteousness. But there are moods in which it unbends. In appealing for help in finding a lost child, for example ('he need not be afraid of returning home' [48]), or in thanking Special Constables 'for the handsome and spirited manner' in which they came forward during the late

unhappy disturbances' [111], it positively beams.

This is the mood in which, historically, the public notice begins to move from admonition to seduction – when it evolves into a new medium altogether: the poster. For commercial purposes, and initially for the pressing purpose of persuading men to join the army [125], the notice begins to appear in less daunting form. Decked out in increasingly attractive finery as affairs become more pressing, it seeks to cajole rather than to admonish. Later, as well as soft words, illustrations begin to appear. Soon the recruiting appeal becomes a work of art; soon the seller of tickets is showing stills from the show.

The development of the poster – the notice with a smile on its face – is another story. But, as in all evolutionary processes, there is an overlap period. In spite of the smile, the commercial announcement and the recruiting appeal continues for a while in Public Notice guise.

The retention of the idiom was due on the one hand to ingrained habit and on the other to enlightened self-interest. The idiom of the public notice, with its advantageous air of Olympian authority, was a tradition not to be sneezed at. For the man who sold his skill as a locksmith [100], or who ran a bus service [108], or a railway [103], the formula carried the weight of centuries of acceptance.

The device continued in use into the twentieth century. Professor Alexander, hypnotist, electrician and bloodless surgeon [212] relied on it in the early 1900s. So, in the same period, did Britain's 1915 campaign 'for those who want to serve their country' [219]. In this instance the three-fold overlap of proclamation, notice and poster appears at its most awkward age; rumbustious in its red and blue lettering, with an 'advertising' headline, and a 'notice' text, it is yet topped and tailed in traditional 'proclamation' style. (The proclamation style died hard. When Kitchener himself moved into the recruiting headline – *Lord Kitchener needs you* – he still insisted on finishing up with *God Save the King*.)

But though the notice evolved into the poster (and afterwards into the purely pictorial poster) it also remained in being in its own right. While the newer medium branched off on its own, the existing one stayed roughly where it was – and where, when occasion demands, it still stands today.

However, it would be wrong to assume that the 'look' of the notice has also remained fixed. There have been a number of more or less clear-cut 'periods'. In the first of these, forerunner of the true notice, the message was painted or incised as a

* *'The well-being of the people is the highest law.'*

one-off individual effort. The Tablets of the Law, set up by the Romans in the Forum, and the hand-written commands of monarchs, are examples.

It was with the advent of printing that the notice proper – and much else – arrived. In the first major phase the 'black letter' of the printer's type dominated. This, a rendering in metal castings of the hand-drawn characters of monastic scribes, remained the standard for upwards of two centuries.

Known also as 'Gothic' and 'Old English', the style has survived into the twentieth century. In its 'bâtarde' form in Germany it had wide currency as an ordinary book and newspaper type even into the 1940s. It had a final fling as a National Socialist 'house-style', and still lingers as a post-war diehard.

In its 'Old English' version it appeared widely in Britain and America as a journal title-piece. Until the mid-1960s its use was virtually standard in the newspaper masthead; it holds out in the 1970s in such unlikely titles as *The Sporting Life* and *The Knoxville Journal*.

The type's most tenacious survival areas are those of law and religion; it is still in brisk demand in ecclesiastical and funerary printing and it appears doggedly, if briefly, in will-forms, contracts, agreements and leases. If the ordinary printed word has authority, for many readers, 'Old English' has it even more so.

Universal as the style was in the fifteenth century, it was soon realized that it was not ideal for the job. New styles of type were devised, more legible and more suitable for the running tempo of the continuous text. Here appeared the beginnings of the typography still in use today. In its letter-forms it abandoned the imitation of handwriting and developed typography as an independent discipline.

In a mayoral declaration published in London in 1684 [3] the two styles appear as a mixture, the 'modern' type, though less bold than the body of the text, serving to add stress to selected words and phrases among the old-style setting.

'Italic', an additional innovation, dates from the early 1500s. This, a sloping or slanting type, was devised in Venice by Aldo Manutio. Though echoing the cursive handwriting of the period, it breaks new ground in its compactness and legibility. In the mayor's announcement already cited [3] it appears in the word *October* in the last line, and in the signature. It also appears (in a later form) as capitals in the printer's footline. In William Shirley's Indian scalp offer of 1755 [4] the mixture of all three styles appears again, with the 'black letter' used only

sparingly and, in this case, largely as stressed rather than unstressed matter.

The new 'book' types were excellent for their purpose. But their use in other forms of printing was less satisfactory. For the public notice, which called for a far more vigorous and compelling effect, they were virtually useless. Even in the largest sizes, normally used only for the most portentous of book title-pages, the types available had a thin and reedy look when used in displayed announcements.

The 'Boy Lost' example already referred to [48], the apology from the Ulverston bottle-thrower [88] and the 'skandalous report' notice [89], are typical; though they attempt to shout, they only whisper.

The 'fat-face' revolution

The notion of 'display' typefaces – the boldly exuberant forms that were to dominate the public notice for a century or more, did not emerge till the early 1800s. Robert Thorne, and his successor William Thorowgood, typefounders and innovators extraordinary, devised typefaces of quite remarkable impact – letters which were so noticeably remote from the tradition of the book that, among ordinary practitioners, they aroused amazement amounting to dismay.

Known as 'fat faces', these types were of the very essence of the public announcement; they could be seen from across the street; they had elegance, character and impact – and they provided the variety of style that an infinite range of subject matter required.

In the present collection, the 'fat faces' predominate. The London Metropolitan Police notice of 1848 [45] and the Lincoln funeral notice of 1865 [172] express the idiom in its heyday. By comparison, their bookish predecessors of the 1700s appear half-hearted and spiritless.

The Thorne and Thorowgood revolution had a far-reaching effect on printing styles. (As the Lincoln announcement indicates, the idea lost nothing in its passage to America.) But the most striking feature of the change was its suddenness. Not only was this the biggest thing to hit printing for some three hundred years, it was also certainly the quickest. Printers who had been sedately chugging along with their book-style layouts suddenly found a whole new typographic world. The effect was galvanizing.

The impact of the change is graphically conveyed in printers' specimen files of the period. In many such collections, in which a single copy of each completed

(*page 15*)

By the Mayor.

To the Alderman of
the Ward of

WHEREAS I have received a RULE, made Yesterday by his MAJESTIES Court of Kings-Bench, whereby (upon great Complaint made to the said Court, That Squibs and Crackers are frequently thrown into Coaches passing the Streets of this CITY, and great mischief thereby done;) It was Ordered, That Warrants be from Me and my Brethren the Aldermen, Issued out to the several Constables of this City, Requiring them to be and attend in the Streets (in their respective Precincts) On the Nine and Twentieth of this instant October, and the Fifth of November next, and the Fifteenth of the said Month of November, to hinder all Persons from throwing Squibs and Crackers in the Streets, and to seize and secure all such as shall presume to throw the same, and not to suffer any Persons whatsoever, either on the Days aforesaid, or at any other Time or Times hereafter, to Throw any Squibs and Crackers into any Coaches in the Streets, but to take Care that all Persons may pass in Coaches quietly and securely without harm or hindrance: And that all Citizens of this City be Aiding and Assisting to the Constables in the Execution of their Office herein.

These are therefore in His MAJESTIES Name streightly to Charge and Require You, immediately to call before You all the several Constables within Your Ward, and give them in strict Charge, That (as They will answer the Contrary at their Perils) They be very careful and diligent to Observe and Execute the said Order: And that They (in their own Persons) give their constant Attendance in and about the Streets, within their respective Precincts, On the said Nine and Twentieth of this Month, and the Fifth and Fifteenth of November next, and there prevent all Throwing of Squibs, and Apprehend all Persons that shall presume to do the same, and bring them before a Justice of the Peace within this City, to be punished according to their Demerits. And that at all other Times likewise, They be watchful to hinder the same; And wherever They shall find any Offending herein, that They fail not to do their Duty in carrying Them before a Justice of the Peace, as aforesaid. And all Citizens and Inhabitants of this City are to Aid and Assist the Constables therein: And hereof I desire You not to fail. Dated the 25th day of October, 1684.

Wagstaffe.

Printed by SAMUEL ROYCROFT, Printer to this Honourable City, 1684.

By His EXCELLENCY

WILLIAM SHIRLEY, Esq;

Captain-General and Governor in Chief, in and over His Majesty's Province of the *Massachusetts-Bay*, in *New-England*, and Vice-Admiral of the same, and Major-General in His Majesty's Army.

A PROCLAMATION.

HEREAS the Indians of *Norridgewock, Arresagun a ook, Weweenock* and *St. John*'s Tribes, and the Indians of the other Tribes inhabiting in the Eastern and Northern Parts of His Majesty's Territories of *New-England*, the *Penobscot* Tribe only excepted, have, contrary to their solemn Submission unto His Majesty long since made and frequently renewed, been guilty of the most perfidious, barbarous and inhuman Murders of divers of his Majesty's *English* Subjects ; and have abstained from all Commerce and Correspondence with His Majesty's said Subjects for many Months past ; and the said *Indians* have fully discovered an inimical, traiterious and rebellious Intention and Disposition ;

I have therefore thought fit to issue this Proclamation, and to Declare the Indians of the Norridgewock, Arresaguntacook, Weweenock and St. John's Tribes, and the Indians of the other Tribes new or late inhabiting in the Eastern and Northren Parts of His Majesty's Territories of New-England, and in Alliance and Confederacy with the above-recited Tribes, the Penobscots only excepted, to be Enemies, Rebels and Traitors to His Most Sacred Majesty: And I do hereby require His Majesty's Subjects of this Province to embrace all Opportunities of pursuing, captivating, killing and destroying all and any of the aforesaid Indians, the Penobscots excepted.

AND WHEREAS the General Court of this Province have voted, That a Bounty or Encouragement be granted and allowed to be paid out of the Publick-Treasury to the marching Army that shall be employed for the Defence of the Eastern and Western Frontiers from the Twenty-fifth of this Month of *June* until the Twenty-fifth of *November* next ;

I have thought fit to publish the same ; and I do hereby promise, That there shall be paid out of the Province-Treasury to all and any of the said Forces, over and above their Bounty upon Enlistment, their Wages and Subsistence, the Premiums or Bounties following, viz.

For every Male Indian Prisoner above the Age of Twelve Years, that shall be taken and brought to *Boston*, *Fifty Pounds.*

For every Male Indian Scalp, brought in as Evidence of their being killed, *Forty Pounds.*

For every Female Indian Prisoner, taken and brought in as aforesaid, and for every Male Indian Prisoner under the Age of Twelve Years, taken and brought in as aforesaid, *Twenty-five Pounds.*

For every Scalp of such Female Indian or Male Indian under Twelve Years of Age, brought as Evidence of their being killed, as aforesaid, *Twenty Pounds.*

GIVEN *under my Hand at* Boston, *in the Province aforesaid, this Twelfth Day of* June, 1755, *and in the Twenty-eighth Year of the Reign of our Sovereign Lord* GEORGE *the Second, by the Grace of* GOD, *of* Great-Britain, France, *and* Ireland, KING, *Defender of the Faith, &c.*

By His Excellency's Command,
J. WILLARD, *Sec'ry.*

W. Shirley.

GOD Save the KING.

BOSTON: Printed by *John Draper*, Printer to His ' the Honourable His Majesty's COUNCIL. 1755.

DUTIES

OF THE

SUPERVISORS, CONSTABLE OF THE NIGHT, AND WATCHMEN,

OF THE PARISH OF

Saint Mary, Islington.

THAT two of the Supervisors do come on duty at sun-set, and remain until twelve o'clock, and then be relieved by the two other, who are to remain on duty until seven o'clock in the morning; this duty to be changed by the Supervisors weekly, in the following manner, (that is to say) the two that come on duty at sun-set, and go off duty at twelve o'clock, to come on duty the following week at twelve o'clock, and remain until seven o'clock in the morning; during the whole of which time they are to be in their respective divisions, by which the Parish will have the advantage of having two Supervisors constantly perambulating.

To keep a Book, and enter every thing that occurs in their respective divisions.

To inspect all Works directed to be done by the Commissioners, and to see them properly performed.

To attend the Commissioners at all their Meetings, and at other times when ordered.

To see the Watchmen go to their respective Beats singly.

To prevent Prostitutes from assembling together, and, as much as possible, prevent them being in this Parish. Also to report to the Magistrates and Commissioners of any Houses kept for the reception of lewd and disorderly persons.

To report to the Magistrates all Publicans who harbour disorderly or dishonest persons, and who do not clear their houses of their company by eleven o'clock at night.

To inspect the Lamps, and make an entry in a Book, to be kept by each of them for that purpose, of the number omitted to be lighted, or shall not continue a-light the whole time specified in the contract, *and to make a return of the same to the Commissioners at every Meeting.*

To see the Watchmen go on and off duty, at their proper times, and while on duty, to see them on their respective beats, awake, and cry the hour; as also while in their boxes, the lanthorns are hung in front of their boxes.

To take care that the Dirt or Rubbish occasioned by building, pulling down, altering, or repairing Houses, be not placed on or near the Footpaths, &c. as to obstruct Carriages or Foot-passengers to pass; and that sufficient light be placed where such Rubbish or Dirt shall be placed, from sun-set to sun-rise, to prevent any mischief happening to Passengers or Cattle.

To prevent any Annoyances in the Footpaths or Streets, &c. *(See Act of Parliament.)*

To prevent Persons exposing to Sale Goods, Wares, &c. on the Footpaths, &c. *(ditto.)*

The Constable of the Night is to set the Watchmen on their duty; to remain in the Watchhouse the whole of the night, until the return of the Watchmen and Supervisors, in order to receive their Reports, and to fairly enter the same in a Book to be kept for that purpose, and that such Book be presented by him every Monday morning to the resident Magistrate, and to the Commissioners at every Meeting. And also that he keep the key of the Watchhouse, and reside as near the same as convenient; and that his Name and Residence be painted on the Watchhouse Door.

The Watchmen to be upon their respective Beats, and not on any account to leave them until the time directed by the Commissioners.

That the Watchmen do make a return of the number of Lamps out, and at what time, in their respective beats, to the Constable of the Night, who is required to enter the same in a Book, to be kept by him for that purpose only, and which Book is not to be inspected by the Supervisors.

By the KING,
A PROCLAMATION.

WILLIAM R.

WHEREAS great multitudes of lawless and disorderly persons have, for some time past, assembled themselves together in a riotous and tumultuous manner, we therefore, being duly sensible of the mischievous consequences which must inevitably ensue, as well to the peace of the kingdom as to the lives and properties of our subjects, from such wicked and illegal practices, if they go unpunished; and being firmly resolved to cause the laws to be put into execution for the punishment of such offenders, have thought fit, by the advice of our Privy Council, to issue this Proclamation, hereby strictly commanding all Justices of the Peace, Sheriffs, Under-Sheriffs, and all other Civil Officers whatsoever, that they do use their utmost endeavours to discover, apprehend, and bring to justice, the persons concerned in the riotous proceedings above-mentioned.

And as a further inducement to discover the said offenders, we do hereby promise and declare that any person or persons who shall discover and apprehend, or cause to be discovered and apprehended, the authors, abettors, or perpetrators of any of the outrages above-mentioned, so that they, or any of them, may be duly convicted thereof, shall be entitled to the sum of

FIFTY POUNDS

for each and every person who shall be convicted, and shall also receive our most gracious pardon for the said offence, in case the person making such discovery as aforesaid shall be liable to be prosecuted for the same.

And whereas certain wicked incendiaries have secretly by FIRE, in many parts destroyed the corn, hay, buildings, and other property of our subjects, we do hereby promise and declare, that any person or persons who shall discover and apprehend, or cause to be discovered and apprehended, the authors of the said fires, so that they, or any of them, may be duly convicted thereof, shall be entitled to the sum of

Five Hundred Pounds

for each and every person who shall be so convicted, and shall also receive our most gracious pardon (except the actual perpetrator of any of the said fires), in case the person making such discovery shall be liable to be prosecuted for the same.

And the Lord Commissioners of our Treasury are hereby required to make payment accordingly of the said rewards.

Given at our Court at St. James's, this twenty-third day of November, one thousand eight hundred aud thirty, in the first year of our reign.

God save the King.

job was mounted in an album for record purposes, the chronological arrangement discloses an abrupt and complete transition. On one page the last of the old style appears, on the next, it seems, with the arrival of a stock of fat-face type, the new begins. There is little or no overlap.

Sometimes however there is a clearly discernible generation gap. Typical is the collection of the work of the Soulby's, father and son, of Ulverston, Barrow-in-Furness.* John Soulby senior (whose 'old style' announcement of apology has already been noted [88]) died in 1817. His work remained old-style to the last. But John Soulby junior, taking up the business where his father left off, did so with a plentiful supply of new type. In the present collection Soulby senior's latest example, his 'Wanton Mischiefs' reward notice [47], appears palid by contrast with his son's 'Gentlemen Sportsmen' warning [86].

The printer as editor

Over and above the impact of the new-style type was the opportunity that its variety gave the printer to express editorial emphasis. The adroit use of type variants had always been part of the printer's expertise. Soulby senior's 'Wanton Mischiefs' item does what it can with contrasts of size, capitals, italics and so forth, but the work of his son's generation offers new dimensions. Examples like Chubb's challenge [100], the 'Popish Priest' election bill [130], and, later, the workhouse notice of 1860 [59] show how the new typography exploits size, style and layout in expressing the message. Often a single phrase or a single word is picked out for special treatment, with each dominant element contributing its full semantic portion.

There is evidence to indicate that printers began to exercise a certain editorial influence over the construction of these items. Limited by the size of the chase – the metal frame in which he set his type – and by availability of types and sizes, the local jobbing printer became familiar with the range of effects he could produce from a given stock of material.

Often, among more modest printers, choice of wording had to be varied to accommodate shortages of particular letters. Often, equally, a line may have been set in a size larger than it merited only because a smaller size was not available, or to fill it out to the full width of the chase.

Although the better printer sought to render his customer's message exactly as supplied, the limitations of the smaller print shop must often have

Now in the Museum of English Rural Life, Reading.

7 Salisbury 1830

8 Blandford 1830

ARREST
THE
MURDERER.

Mr. Charles Butler was most brutally murdered this morning, on the Washington road 2 miles West of this place, by one John Hide, who has escaped and made his way to parts unknown. Said Hide is about 5 feet 10 or 11 inches high, about 35 years of age, weighs 150 or 160 lbs., fair skin, blue eyes, large mouth, and is rather talkative; he rode off a chesnut sorrel horse, (a stallion.) His brother, a heavier man, complexion much the same, left in company with him, riding a mule.

The murder being of such a cold-blooded and outrageous character, the neighbors authorize me to say a large reward, exclusive of the regular lawful reward, will be given for the apprehension of said Hide.

Houston, Feb. 1, 1852.3   J. B. HOGAN, *Sheriff of Harris County*

9 Houston 1853

NOTICE.

IT is strongly suspected, that most of the FIRES have been caused by TWO MEN, who have been seen near the Spot either a short time before, or immediately after their breaking out. They have been making enquiries of Shepherds and Labourers respecting the Situations of Farms, and different Circumstances relating to them.

One is about 40 Years of Age, rides a long-legged, light-carcassed, sorrel-coloured Horse, what is vulgarly called a Blood Horse, with a Switch Tail; wears Knee-caps or Over-alls, sometimes has a Drab Great Coat; generally is seen riding fast through Villages or Towns, with something different from a common riding Stick, with which he is constantly striking the Horse's Off-Shoulder.

The other rides a Black Horse, of the same long-legged Description: they are dressed and look like Farmers. It is supposed that the thing which is carried in the Hand is an Air Gun, from which a small Shell is thrown, which ignites after a certain time.

It is supposed that in Dorset, the Incendiaries are travelling on foot in different disguises, making the same enquiries as above.

SHIPP, PRINTER, BLANDFORD.

TEN
POUNDS
REWARD.

Whereas,

**Certain evil disposed, and strongly sus-
pected Persons, have recently committed
divers nightly Trespasses & Depredations
on WICK GROUNDS, in the Parish of
Brislington.**

NOTICE

**Is hereby given, that whoever will give
such information as may lead to the Conviction of one or more of the said Offenders,
shall thereon receive the**

Reward of 10 Pounds

**on application to WILLIAM WITHERING,
Esquire, at Wick House.**

N.B. Extra Patrols

*are now appointed for the protection of
the above-mentioned Premises; and
whoever shall be taken into custody so
offending, will be prosecuted with the
utmost rigour of the Law.*

Dec. 29th, 1830.

R. BARRY, PRINTER, HIGH-STREET, BRISTOL.

11 Bristol 1830

WHEREAS
TWO PERSONS

**Wearing Dark Great Coats and Hats
with *Broad Brims*, were about four
o'Clock on Sunday Morning *last* seen
near the Hedge between Mill Down and
one of Mr. Coward's *Wheat Fields*, who
on being discovered immediately ran towards
the Lane leading to Shaftesbury; *and whereas***
It is *strongly suspected* that such Two Persons were concerned
in *setting Fire to the Ricks* belonging to Mr. Christopher Good,
and Mr. John White; Any Person who might at the time before
mentioned have seen *Two Men* answering the above Description
will *much further the Cause of Justice* by communicating the fact
to the Bailiff of the Borough of Blandford.
*N. B. The Persons described appeared to be Young Men above the Lower Class
of Society.*   Blandford, 29th November, 1828.

SHIPP, PRINTER, BLANDFORD.

12 Blandford 1828

dictated detail of layout, emphasis and wording. It may be assumed that on a majority of occasions the customer would present himself personally at the printers – sometimes without benefit of a prepared text. Just as the small-advertisement customer of today will often accept the advice of his local newspaper in wording an announcement, the jobbing printer's customer similarly 'left it to the expert'. It was in situations like these, where the printer sought to strengthen his customer's message to the full, that *Whereas*'s and *By Orders* tended to multiply. (We may visualise Mrs Tuck of Oxford Street [89] at the counter of the Catnach establishment in Seven Dials as the proprietor himself drafted the terms of her complaint – starting with a new-style fat-face heading and an old-style statutory *Whereas*. The spelling, and the misprint, are clearly also his own unaided work.)

The printer as designer

The matter of layout and emphasis in the public notice is no small matter. As with newspaper typography, the aim is to convey the whole story, forcefully and briefly, avoiding as far as possible long passages of unrelieved text, and breaking the message into commanding and easily assimilable sections. In its ideal form the public notice stresses key words and phrases so as to convey an immediate telegraphic impact. Subsidiary clauses and qualifying phrases may be left for detailed reading after the main message has been grasped.

The Mile End Old Town workhouse notices [56, 57, 58, 59] though overloaded with a multiplicity of typefaces, are all good examples of the telegraphic approach. Noticeably less successful in this is the Ilion funeral announcement [172]: *Business be closed* is not a phrase that serves as a logical stepping stone from the heading to the bold lines below. Nor does *Religious Services!*, even with the inducement of an exclamation mark, do well as a punch-line.

Here, (though again the misprint is the printer's own contribution) the text has been drafted by the customer without regard to its possibilities as print. Too timid, or too ignorant, to suggest changes in wording, the printer has done what he could with a text that does not lend itself to display treatment.

Something of the same difficulty appears in the Kennington Common meeting item [45]. In a display that maintains its linguistic and typographic rationale through a dozen lines or so, there is an apparent collapse around the half-way mark. At this point, where a section of small type breaks into a *(page 22)*

BURGLARY
And Felony.
120 Pounds
REWARD.

Whereas on Sunday Night the 25th inst. or early on the following Morning, the Dwelling-House of MORGAN YEATMAN, Esq. situate in the Borough of Dorchester, was burglariously entered and a number of Silver Articles and several Pounds in Money stolen therefrom:

Any Person (whether an Accomplice or not) who will give Information so that the Offender or Offenders may be convicted, shall, on such conviction, receive a Reward of TWENTY POUNDS, by applying to Mr. FRANCIS INGRAM, Secretary of the Dorchester Association for the Protection of Persons and Property, and also the further Reward of ONE HUNDRED POUNDS, (subscribed by the Town at large) by applying to the Mayor.

Dorchester, November 28th, 1821.

G. CLARK, PRINTER, DORCHESTER.

13 Dorchester 1821

£300
REWARD.

WHEREAS about 8 o'clock on the Morning of
Wednesday, 7th July inst.
A Daring Attempt
was made by Three Men in Mitre Court, Wood Street, Cheapside, to rob the *Lombard Street*
LETTER CARRIER
Of the Letters he was proceeding to deliver; he was knocked down and severely beaten with a Life Preserver, which was found near the spot.

Whoever will give such Information as shall lead to the Apprehension and Conviction of the Offenders, shall be entitled to a Reward of
Three Hundred Pounds
payable on Conviction.

Apply to M. B. Peacock, Esq., Solicitor, General Post Office, London.

General Post Office, 7th July, 1847.

14 London 1847

18

TEN POUNDS
REWARD.

Whereas several Anonymous Letters have lately been sent to a respectable Inhabitant of St. Mary-at-Hill, containing charges injurious to the character of the Parties therein-named. The above Reward will be paid to any Person giving such Information as may lead to the Discovery and Conviction of the Offender or Offenders, on application to Mr. Lawless, Stationer, 24, Little Eastcheap.

OCT. 30, 1829.

Lawless, Printer, Little Eastcheap.

15 London 1829

Whereas between the hours of 3 o'clock and 7, on the afternoon of Friday, November 24th, some evil disposed person or persons
DID STEAL A CERTAIN
BRASS CROSS
From the Communion Table of Holy Trinity Church; a
REWARD
OF £3
Will be given to anyone who will give such information as will lead to the conviction of the Offender or Offenders

16 London (?) *c* 1860

V R.

£8000 REWARD

ROBBERY and MURDER.

WHEREAS EDWARD KELLY, DANIEL KELLY, STEPHEN HART, and JOSEPH BYRNE have been declared OUTLAWS in the Colony of Victoria, and whereas warrants have been issued charging the aforesaid men with the WILFUL MURDER of MICHAEL SCANLON, Police Constable of the Colony of VICTORIA, and whereas the above-named offenders are STILL at LARGE and have recently committed divers felonies in the Colony of NEW SOUTH WALES: Now, therefore, I, SIR HERCULES GEORGE ROBERT ROBINSON, the GOVERNOR, do, by this, my proclamation issued with the advice of the Executive Council, hereby notify that a REWARD of £4,000 will be paid, three-fourths by the Government of NEW SOUTH WALES, and one-fourth by certain Banks trading in the Colony, for the apprehension of the above-named Four Offenders, or a reward of £1000 for the apprehension of any one of them, and that in ADDITION to the above reward, a similar REWARD of £4000 has been offered by the Government of VICTORIA, and I further notify that the said REWARD will be equitably apportioned between any persons giving information which shall lead to the apprehension of the offenders and any members of the police force or other persons who may actually effect such apprehension or assist thereat.

(Signed) HENRY PARKES,
Colonial Secretary, New South Wales.

(Signed) BRYAN O'LOGHLEN,
Attorney General, Victoria.

Dated 15th February, 1879.

17 Victoria/New South Wales 1879

50 POUNDS
REWARD.

Whereas, Three several Fires have occurred within the last fortnight in the Parish of Blandford St. Mary, in the County of Dorset., which there is too much reason to believe were the work of an Incendiary.

The above Reward will be given to any Person or Persons giving such information, privately or otherwise, as to either of the said Fires as may lead to the discovery of the perpetrator.

The above Reward will only be paid on the Conviction of the Offender.

Dated, Down House, Sep. 4, 1850.   J. W. SMITH, BART.

W. SHIPP, PRINTER, BLANDFORD.

18 Blandford 1850

ROBBERY
£25 REWARD.

WHEREAS the Dwelling House of T. B. ESSERY, Esq., situate in Gloucester Place, Swansea, was, between the hours of six and half-past seven on the evening of Saturday, the 14th of November last, feloniously entered by some party or parties unknown, and a Dressing Case containing Money and Jewellery, and other Property, to the value of Seventy Pounds taken therefrom, part of which property has since been recovered, but there yet remain the following articles stolen, viz:—

£12 in gold and a few shillings.
A small Ruby Brooch, star shaped, interspersed with pearls.
A Gold Watch Pin.
A Gold Ring, set with a diamond in centre, encircled with pearls.
A Chased Gold Ring.
Two long Gold Pins, twisted for the hair.
Six handsome Malachite Studs set in gold, contained in a long leather case.
Silver Fittings of Dressing Case.
A large wash-leather Purse, with gold snaps.
A long Silver Hairpin, with pearl top.
A small Thermometer, about an inch long, ornamented in gold and steel, with a cornelian seal at bottom.
A small Sovereign Purse of grey silk, with a fringe of steel beads.
A grey leather Purse, bound with steel.
Two Glass Bottles belonging to Dressing Case.

This is therefore to give Notice that the above Reward will be paid by the Swansea Association for Prosecuting Felons to any person giving such information as shall lead to the Apprehension and Conviction of the Offender or Offenders.

C. K. McADAM, Secretary.

Swansea, Dec. 16th, 1857.

PRINTED AT THE CAMBRIAN OFFICE, SWANSEA.

19 Swansea 1857

19

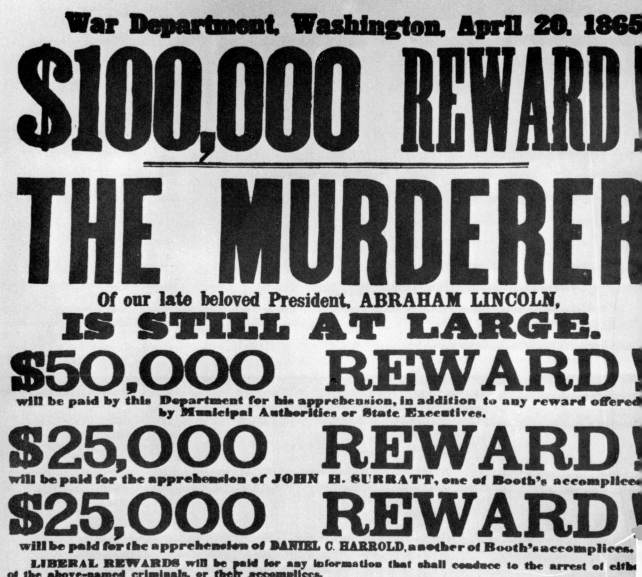

War Department, Washington, April 20, 1865

$100,000 REWARD!

THE MURDERER

Of our late beloved President, ABRAHAM LINCOLN,

IS STILL AT LARGE.

$50,000 REWARD!

will be paid by this Department for his apprehension, in addition to any reward offered by Municipal Authorities or State Executives.

$25,000 REWARD!

will be paid for the apprehension of JOHN H. SURRATT, one of Booth's accomplices.

$25,000 REWARD!

will be paid for the apprehension of DANIEL C. HARROLD, another of Booth's accomplices.

LIBERAL REWARDS will be paid for any information that shall conduce to the arrest of either of the above-named criminals, or their accomplices.

All persons harboring or secreting the said persons, or either of them, or aiding or assisting their concealment or escape, will be treated as accomplices in the murder of the President and the attempted assassination of the Secretary of State, and shall be subject to trial before a Military Commission and the punishment of DEATH.

Let the stain of innocent blood be removed from the land by the arrest and punishment of the murderers.

All good citizens are exhorted to aid public justice on this occasion. Every man should consider his own conscience charged with this solemn duty, and rest neither night nor day until it be accomplished.

EDWIN M. STANTON, *Secretary of War.*

DESCRIPTIONS.—BOOTH is 5 feet 7 or 8 inches high, slender build, high forehead, black hair, black eyes, and wears a heavy black moustache.
JOHN H. SURRATT is about 5 feet 9 inches. Hair rather thin and dark; eyes rather light; no beard. Would weigh 145 or 150 pounds. Complexion rather pale and clear, with color in his cheeks. Wore light clothes of fine quality. Shoulders square; check bones rather prominent; chin narrow; ears projecting at the top; head rather low and square, but broad. Parts his hair on the right side; neck rather long. His lips are firmly set. A slim man.
DANIEL C. HARROLD is 22 years of age, 5 feet 6 or 7 inches high, rather broad shouldered, otherwise light built; dark hair, little (if any) moustache; dark eyes; weighs about 140 pounds.

RESCUE.

5 Guineas Reward.

WHEREAS one JOHN CREARY, was, on Sunday the 29th August, Instant, apprehended on a Charge of RIOT and DRUNKENNESS, and lodged in an Appartment of Dalton Castle in safe Custody during the Night, from whence he was Released, by some evil disposed Person or Persons unknown.

NOTICE
Is Hereby Given,

That a Reward of FIVE GUINEAS, will be paid to any Person, who will give such Information to the Constables of Dalton, as shall lead to the Apprehension and Conviction of the Person or Persons, who released the said JOHN CREARY from Custody.

Dalton in Furness, August 30th, 1824.

———ooo0ooo———

J. Soulby, Printer, Market Place, Ulverston.

4 Ulverston 1824

25 GUINEAS
REWARD.

Henfield Prosecuting Society.

WHEREAS some evil disposed Person or Persons, did, in the Night of Tuesday, the 8th Instant, break open the Stable on Furzefield Farm, in the Parish of Shermanbury, in the occupation of Mr. THOMAS PAGE, and maliciously CUT OFF and carry away

THE HAIR
FROM THE
TAILS OF 3 CART HORSES
the property of the said THOMAS PAGE.
A REWARD OF
FIVE GUINEAS

will be given to any Person or Persons giving Information of the Offender or offenders, so that he or they may be Convicted thereof, such Reward to be paid by the Treasurer of the said Society, immediately after such Conviction.

THOMAS COPPARD, Clerk.

HORSHAM, 9th MAY, 1838.

A FURTHER REWARD OF

20 GUINEAS
will be paid on such Conviction as aforesaid, by me

THOMAS PAGE.

Printed by Charles Hunt, West Street, Horsham.

22 Henfield 1838

MURDER
Of Police, near Mansfield.
£2000 !!
REWARD.
For Capture of offenders Kellys, and two others, increased to £500 for each offender.

THE FOUR OFFENDERS ARE OUTLAWED

By order

Manly Ellis,

372 S.C. POLICE.

24 Jamieson, Victoria 1878

London, Brighton and South Coast Railway.

D. 4299.

£10 REWARD

Whereas, on Sunday, the 13th March, 1892, it was found on examination that Three Carriages (Nos. 169 First and 316 and 321 Second Class) standing in the Sidings at Norwood Junction, had been wilfully and maliciously damaged by some unknown evil-disposed person or persons, 17 cushions being cut open and the horse hair stolen, the Directors hereby give notice that the above Reward of Ten Pounds will be paid to anyone who shall furnish such information as will lead to the conviction of the offender or offenders.

(By Order) **A. SARLE,**
Secretary & General Manager.

LONDON BRIDGE TERMINUS, *March*, 1892.

Waterlow and Sons Limited, Printers, London Wall, London.

26 London 1892

REWARD
five hundred dollars

TO THE LOYAL CITIZENS OF TENNESSEE:

A Yankee Spy is in your midst Thomas, the invader has sent among you a spy, who is expected to betray the Confederate armies and the State of Tennessee into his hands. Be on the alert. The Spy is one MAY MERTON, a girl about 19 years of age, born near Chattanooga. She is therefore familiar with the country into which she has been sent. She is supposed to be lurking somewhere in the neighborhood of Morgan's or Longstreet's camp.

A reward of Five Hundred Dollars in Gold will be paid by the Confederate Government at Richmond, Va., or by Generals Morgan, Longstreet and Bragg, for the apprehension of this spy, dead or alive. Confederate Loyal People of Tennessee, hunt down this notorious woman, and when captured let her be treated to the rope she so richly merits. Once more I ask you to be on the alert.

By order of

JEFFERSON DAVIS, President C.S.A.
JUDAH P. BENJAMIN, Secretary of State.
GEORGE W. RANDOLF, Secretary of War.

3 Tennessee 1861

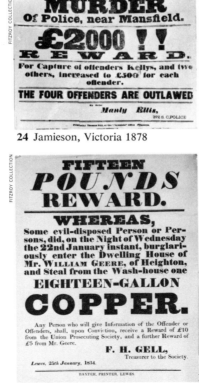

FIFTEEN
POUNDS
REWARD.
WHEREAS,
Some evil-disposed Person or Persons, did, on the Night of Wednesday the 22nd January instant, burglariously enter the Dwelling House of Mr. WILLIAM GEERE, of Heighton, and Steal from the Wash-house one

EIGHTEEN-GALLON
COPPER.

Any Person who will give Information of the Offender or Offenders, shall, upon Conviction, receive a Reward of £10 from the Union Prosecuting Society, and a further Reward of £5 from Mr. Geere.

F. H. GELL,
Treasurer to the Society.

Lewes, 25th January, 1834.

BAXTER, PRINTER, LEWES.

25 Lewes 1834

300 dollars
REWARD!!

STOLEN from my Lot in the Town of Columbus, Colorado County, Texas, on the night of the 10th of January, 1867, a

STALLION

of the following description, viz: Six years old the coming spring, 15 1-2 hands high, Dark Bay color, Black Tail, and Black Mane which lies on the left side of the neck; *Curl* in the hair on the *right* side of the neck, about *midway*, near the mane; *Star* in the forehead about the size of a dollar, *elongated* up and down; Bay Hairs *mixed* with the white throughout, about *half-and-half*; *White* above the *right* hind foot, extending above the fetlock—one little Black Spot the size of a *half dime* on *each side*, just above the Hoof, which is striped *black* and *white*; *White* above the left fore-hoof, on the inner or right side, extending *up* about two inches, but does not extend to the outer or left side of the hoof—two small *black* spots, about the size of a half dime, just above the edge of the hoof, on the right or white side—outer left side of hoof *black*, inside *white* and *black*. The above-described

HORSE

was raised by Mr. H. D. RHODES, of this County, and was trained by Mr. COWLEY, at Mr. HARPER'S, in Lavaca County.

☞ $100 will be given for the horse returned *uninjured*, and $200 for proof to convict the thief.

C. W. TAIT.

27 Columbus, Texas 1867

$1,000 Reward!
WE WILL PAY FIVE HUNDRED DOLLARS FOR THE
Arrest and Detention
UNTIL HE CAN BE REACHED, OF

Tom Nixon,

Alias TOM BARNES, five feet seven or eight inches high, 145 to 150 lbs. weight, 25 years of age, blue-gray eyes, light hair and whiskers; beard not heavy or long; mustache older and longer than beard. He is a blacksmith, and worked at that trade in the Black Hills, last summer; has friends in Minnesota and Indiana. He was one of the robbers of the Union Pacific Train, at Big Springs, Nebraska, on September 18, 1877.

He had about $10,000 in $20 Gold pieces of the stolen money in his possession, of the coinage of the San Francisco Mint of 1877. The above reward will be paid for his arrest and detention, and 10 per cent. of all moneys recovered; previous rewards as regards him are withdrawn.

ANY INFORMATION LEADING TO HIS APPREHENSION WILL BE REWARDED. Address,

ALLAN PINKERTON,
191 and 193 Fifth Avenue,   CHICAGO, ILLINOIS.
Or, **E. M. MORSMAN,**
Supt. U. P. R. R. Express,   OMAHA, NEBRASKA.

28 Chicago/Omaha 1877

single larger line (NUMBERS OF PEOPLE, NOR AT ANY ONE TIME WITH ABOVE THE NUMBER OF) the printer appears to lose his grip. Overcome, perhaps, by the mass of wording still to be fitted into the remaining space, he seems to have finished it off more or less as it fell out.

It is not to be wondered at that, with some three hundred words of text to jam in, and with only a few days in which to do the job (and with Messrs Rowan and Mayne breathing down his neck as he worked), this *tour de force* gave out in the middle.

Even as a leisured piece of setting, it may be imagined how difficult an exercise a job of this kind may be. Working with only a handwritten draft (itself possibly amended and re-amended), with more or less arbitrary underscorings of the customer, it is virtually impossible to predict the final appearance of the completed work.

In the long run, printers allowed the principle of multiple type-change to run away with them. Towards the latter part of the century, what had begun as a rational principle became a habit. Ultimately display printing everywhere was to degenerate into a pointless potpourri of typefaces and sizes. But in its prime, nothing could detract from the typographic glory of the printed notice. The jobbing printer had evolved an idiom which was to endure: the 'public notice' style. In general principles it remains unchanged today.

Rewards, riots and reform

The files of the local jobbing printer serve as evidence not only of typographic trends but of history. In the small, close-knit communities of the early nineteenth century, one repository of public record was the local newspaper; the other, parenthetic and often ignored, was the printed notice. For the most part, not surprisingly, the subject matter is Law and Order; the detail is of crime and punishment.

Pre-eminent among the law-and-order uses of the public notice is the offering of rewards. If money has loomed large in the history of crime, it has also played no small part in detection; the Establishment has never shrunk from exploiting the acquisitiveness that makes thieves for the purpose of catching them.

The reward is a dubious instrument. Though at first sight merely an offer by open-handed Authority to a law-abiding Public, it is in reality a straightforward bribe – an offer to accomplices to profit at the expense of their colleagues. Though cloaked in an air of righteousness, it comes perilously close to (*page 26*)

REWARD!

WELLS, FARGO & CO'S

Express was Robbed this Morning, between Ione Valley and Galt, by two men, described as follows:

One elderly, heavy set, and sandy complexion. The other tall, slim, and dark complexion.

$200 Each and one-fourth of the Treasure recovered, will be paid for the *arrest* and *conviction* of the robbers.

JNO. J. VALENTINE, Gen. Supt.

San Francisco, May 3d, 1875.

29 San Francisco 1875

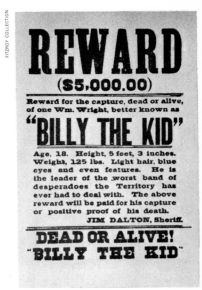

REWARD
($5,000.00)

Reward for the capture, dead or alive, of one Wm. Wright, better known as

"BILLY THE KID"

Age, 18. Height, 5 feet, 3 inches. Weight, 125 lbs. Light hair, blue eyes and even features. He is the leader of the worst band of desperadoes the Territory has ever had to deal with. The above reward will be paid for his capture or positive proof of his death.

JIM DALTON, Sheriff.

DEAD OR ALIVE!
"BILLY THE KID"

30 Lincoln 1877

FIVE HUNDRED DOLLARS
REWARD!

WELLS, FARGO & CO.
WILL PAY

FIVE HUNDRED DOLLARS,

For the arrest and conviction of the robber who stopped the Quincy Stage and demanded the Treasury Box, on Tuesday afternoon, August 17th, near the old Live Yankee Ranch, about 17 miles above Oroville. By order of

J. J. VALENTINE, Gen'l Supt.

Oroville, August 18, 1875.   RIDEOUT, SMITH & CO., Agents.

31 Oroville 1875

REWARD!

WELLS, FARGO & Co.'s EXPRESS BOX, on Chinese and Copperopolis Stage, was ROBBED this morning, by one man about two miles from Burns Ferry. (Ruplee's Bridge,) Tuolumne county side, of $600 in coin and gold dust.

For arrest and conviction of the Robber, we will pay $300, and one-fourth of any portion of treasure recovered.

ROBBER described as follows: A Mexican, lightish complexion, rather short and thick set; weight about 150 lbs.; had a moustache and short growth of beard.

San Francisco, Dec. 1. 1875.   TUOLUMNE INDEPENDENT PRINT.

JOHN J. VALENTINE,
General Superintendent.

32 San Francisco 1875

HEADQUARTERS SOUTHERN INDIANA,

VIGILANCE COMMITTEE.

TO THE PEOPLE OF THE UNITED STATES!

"SALUS POPULI SUPREMA LEX."

WHEREAS, it became necessary for this organization to meet out summary punishment to the leaders of the thieves, robbers, murderers and desperadoes, who for many years defied law and order, and threatened the lives and property of honest citizens of this portion of Indiana, and as the late fearful tragedy at New Albany testifies that justice is slow, but sure, we promulgate this our pronunciamento, for the purpose of justifying to the world, and particularly to the people of the State of Indiana, any future action which we may take.

We deeply deplore the necessity which called our organization into existence; but the laws of our State are so defective that as they now stand on the Statute Books, they all favor criminals going unwhipt of justice; a retrospective view will show that in this respect we speak only the truth.

Having first lopped off the branches, and finally uprooted the tree of evil which was in our midst, in defiance of us and our laws, we beg to be allowed to rest here, and be not forced again to take the law into our own hands. We are very loth to shed blood again, and will not do so unless compelled in defence of our lives.

A WARNING.

We are well aware that at the present time, a combination of the few remaining thieves, their friends and sympathizers, has been formed against us, and have threatened all kinds of vengeance against persons whom they suppose to belong to this organization. They threaten assassination in every form, and that they will commit arson in such ways as will defy legal detection. The carrying out in whole, or in part, of each or any of these designs, is the only thing that will again cause us to rise in our own defence. The following named persons are solemnly warned, that their designs and opinions are known, and that they cannot, unknown to us, make a move toward retaliation.

Wilk Reno, Clinton Reno, Trick Reno, James Greer, Stephen Greer, Fee Johnson, Chris. Price, Harvey Needham, Meade Fislar, Mart Lowe, Roland Lee, William Sparks, Jesse Thompson, William Hare, William Biggers, James Fislar, Pollard Able.

If the above named individuals desire to remain in our midst, to pursue honest callings, and otherwise conduct themselves as law abiding citizens, we will protect them always.— If however, they commence their devilish designs against us, our property, or any good citizen of this district, we will rise but *once* more ; do not trifle with us ; for if you do, we will follow you to the bitter end; and give you a "short shrift and a hempen collar." As to this, our actions in the past, will be a guarantee for our conduct in the future.

We trust this will have a good effect. We repeat, we are very loth again to take life, and hope we shall never more be necessitated to take the law into our own hands.

By order of the Committee.

Dec. 21, 1868.

$150 REWARD!
BROKE JAIL!

WILLIAM RAVENSCRAFT, American, light hair, about 5 feet 10 inches high, genteel dress, thin in flesh, has a crease in his under lip, about 28 years of age.

Also, **WILLIAM ELLIS**, American, dark complexion, thin in the face, about 32 years old, 5 feet 6 inches high, large hazel eye, had on when he left a black hat, broad check pants of a light blue color.

Also, **WILLIAM DETHRO**, American, dark complexion, about 5 feet 9 inches, medium size, strong in his appearance, had on when he left blue and white check pants, blue stripe running round, and a jeans frock coat, and rather a broad brimed felt hat, high crown, dented in at the top, considerably worn.

$50 will be paid for either one, or **$150** for the three, delivered to the Chicago Jail. **$25** for any private information of either of the above described.

I. COOK, Sheriff Cook County.

Chicago, August 4th, 1847.

34 Chicago 1847

PROCLAMATION.

BY THE GOVERNOR OF THE TERRITORY OF OREGON.

In pursuance of an Act of Congress, approved on the fourteenth day of August, in the year of our Lord one thousand eight hundred and forty-eight, establishing a Territorial Government in the Territory of Oregon :—

I, Joseph Lane, was on the eighteenth day of August, in the year eighteen hundred and forty-eight, commissioned Governor in and for the Territory of Oregon. I have therefore thought proper to issue this my Proclamation, making known that I have this day entered upon the discharge of the duties of my office, and by virtue thereof do declare that the Laws of the United States are extended over, and declared to be in force in said Territory, so far as the same, or any portion thereof may be applicable.

Given under my hand, at Oregon City, in the Territory of Oregon, this third day of March, Anno Domini 1849.

JOSEPH LANE.

35 Oregon City 1849

REWARD
$10,000
IN GOLD COIN

Will be paid by the U. S. Government for the apprehension

DEAD OR ALIVE
of
SAM and BELLE STARR

Wanted for Robbery, Murder, Treason and other acts against the peace and dignity of the U. S.

THOMAS CRAIL
Major, 8th Missouri Cavalry, Commanding

36 Younger's Bend, Arkansas 1886

WIGAN COUNTY BOROUGH POLICE.

STOLEN,
From the person of a Gentleman in this Borough on the 31st of March last,

A GENT'S GOLD LEVER
CENTRE-SECONDS STOP-WATCH

Cream-coloured dial, No. 15108, maker: John Seddon, Wigan.

The following inscription engraved on inner case :—" Presented to James Fairhurst, by his beloved Wife, on his Birthday."

Had attached a 9ct. Gold Albert Chain, fancy link pattern, with a Queen Anne Guinea as a pendant.

Please cause enquiries to be made of Pawnbrokers, Watchmakers, and others, and if found, communicate with

Chief Constable's Office, Wigan, April 4th, 1893.   **Captain A. BELL, Chief Constable.**

37 Wigan 1893

GENERAL POST OFFICE

£1,000
REWARD
ROBBERY

at 7.45 p.m. 24th February, 1968
from Paddington Head District Post Office,
London W.2

The Postmaster General intends to pay a reward or rewards up to a total of £1000 to any person or persons giving information which, in the opinion of The Postmaster General, shall lead to the apprehension and the conviction of the persons responsible for this robbery. The amount of any payment will be entirely in the discretion of The Postmaster General and applications for consideration should be addressed to him and sent to the General Post Office, London.

Information about the robbery should be given to New Scotland Yard. Tel: 01-230 1212, or at any police station.

38 London 1968

MALICIOUS DAMAGE
and hooliganism

Most passengers are law-abiding and consider the comfort of others. Sporting crowds - football supporters, for instance - are in general well-behaved. It is only a tiny minority who spoil the day's enjoyment for others.

For this minority, here is a warning: DO NOT CAUSE DAMAGE TO TRAINS or other London Transport property. The penalties are severe - up to £100 or 3 MONTHS IMPRISONMENT - and they are even heavier if accidents or injuries are caused, or are likely to be caused. THINK FIRST - IT JUST ISN'T WORTH IT!

London Transport is grateful for help. Please report any damage you see done, with details, as soon as you can. Up to £50 reward may be paid for information leading to a conviction.

39 London 1968

REWARD

THE LONDON CLEARING BANKS will, until further notice, pay a reward of up to £2,500 to any member of the public who gives information to the Police leading to the conviction of any person for stealing or attempting or conspiring to steal any of their property, wherever it may be, in the United Kingdom, or for breaking into any of their branches in the United Kingdom with intent to steal.

1st NOVEMBER, 1971

40 London 1971

the levels it affects to condemn. It is also an admission of helplessness; as an undeniably *post facto* expedient it is as much an advertisement for successful lawlessness as for the law. Where reward notices flourish, the honest citizen does well to bar his doors.

In no area did the reward notice proliferate as readily as it did in the early American West. Resplendent in new-style typography, it was as common a feature of the New America as the gambling hell, the saloon and the sheriff's office.

Though never lacking in vigour, its design and layout reached full maturity in the 1870s. The advent of Henry Wells and William Fargo, with the opportunities offered by in-transit treasury and bullion, provided frequent subject matter.

1875 was a typical year. John J Valentine, Wells Fargo's general superintendent, had a thin time [32]. His offers of rewards as high as one quarter of the value of treasure retrieved – in addition to big conviction payments – show little faith in his prospects of success. On the whole, his pessimism was justified.

(This was the period, incidentally, in which the name of one Allan Pinkerton emerged as a signatory of reward offers [28]. Flexing his muscles on counterfeit gangs and railway thieves in the forties and fifties, Pinkerton had moved into Wells Fargo country after organizing intelligence in the Civil War. His 'National Detective Agency' was to form the nucleus of the Federal Secret Service.)

The reward system is not only an instrument of doubtful morality, it has the more pressing disadvantage of not being a very good one. Often it has proved completely useless. The Ned Kelly reward of £8,000 in 1879 [17] is a case in point. Popular sympathy for Kelly was reward-proof. No one, among the many hundreds who knew his whereabouts, gave him away. Similarly in Britain in the 1830s (when the penalty for machine-wrecking was seven years transportation and the penalty for rick-burning was death) big rewards were offered for 'information'. The king's offer of five hundred pounds [6], at that time a substantial sum, was later raised to one thousand pounds. No one ever claimed either sum.

Though first to meet the eye, the reward notice is only a section of the jobbing printer's repertoire. The range is wide.

Typical, and sharply indicative of their period, are the public notices of Dorset. Many scores of these have survived; like the Ulverston collection, they are culled from specimen files of local printers. Many are now preserved as exhibits in the Dorset County

Museum. They chronicle much of the county's social history, from the invasion scare at the beginning of the century to the closing of hotels and public houses on the day of Queen Victoria's funeral. The small selection reproduced here covers subjects as diverse as Tippling during Divine Service [138], the Abolition of Christmas Boxes [105] and Aid to Refugees [49].

But the Dorset collection does more than record the affairs of one small locality; it encapsulates the social history of the century.

In Britain the early 1800s had provided fertile ground for apprehension. Developing technology, new economic conditions – and an Establishment that saw no reason to modify eighteenth-century social patterns – combined at the turn of the century to produce smouldering unrest. The agricultural labourer, who had till now provided the power supply of an agrarian economy, found his livelihood at risk. With wage rates apparently frozen for good at eighteenth-century levels, with rising prices adding to already intolerable poverty, and with mechanization threatening to do him out of a job altogether, he turned on his master.

It was the coming of the threshing machine in the 1820s (part of the same advancing technology that had brought John Soulby junior his new iron printing press) that brought things to a head. The work of threshing, hitherto a means for a man to earn marginally more than his average of nine shillings a week, was suddenly denied him.

'Nightly tumultuous assemblages'

There had been disturbance, on and off, in various parts of the country. In 1795 and in 1816 there had been violence and sporadic outbreaks of rick-burning. On 29 August 1830, trouble started again in earnest. Four hundred Kent farm workers destroyed a number of threshing machines. In a short time, much of the South was in a state of near-insurrection. Dorset, and neighbouring counties, became centres of violent protest.

The forces of Law and Order, none too sure of themselves, rallied. Magistrates and soldiery moved in. 'Special Commissions' sat in judgement. (These, themselves not undaunted by possibilities of violence, sought the protection of special constables [7]). In mass hearings, the delinquents were tried and sentenced. As a result, from a total of thirteen counties, Law and Order delivered 457 agricultural labourers to transportation and six to the scaffold.

At every stage the public notice marked the day. It served not only in official capacity; private persons, farmers, landed gentry, and others with property interests, also went into print.

Some of these, seeking to discount the spontaneity of popular opinion, cast about for 'outside influences' as source of the troubles. One Douglas Stuart, 'A Special Constable', congratulated his fellow specials on the quelling of a lawless rabble and opined that the incendiary and insubordinate would not again have the temerity to cross the Dorsetian border [8]. In another notice, published by five Blandford Justices of the Peace, citizens were warned against attempts of 'wicked persons who are known to be in the neighbouring Counties' and who would seize any opportunity of 'extending to this District the ravages of Fire . . .'

The gambit was not an unfamiliar one; similar notices had appeared before. In these it was claimed that 'strangers' had been seen in the neighbourhoods concerned. Small groups of trouble-makers, it seemed, were moving through the countryside from county to county, firing ricks, farm buildings and crops. In a number of private-sector notices detailed descriptions of these persons appeared: 'They are dressed and look like farmers' [10]; '. . . appeared to be Young Men above the Lower Class of Society' [12]. It must be said that some of the descriptions failed to ring entirely true.

In 1831 further notices continue the story of protest and unrest. On 12 April Blandford magistrates announce the return of Law and Order. With tranquility 'now happily restored', they congratulate everyone all round and forthwith dismiss their special constables [111]. But less than a month later comes the election. This, fought on the issue of Reform, is marked by more violence [112, 113] and in October, with the second rejection of the Reform Bill (by the House of Lords) another crop of notices records the effects of rioting.

Among premises broken into, with 'Deeds, Writings, Papers or Books . . . scattered about the Streets' [116] is the shop of Mr Shipp, printer of notices, no less, who puts out his own appeal [114] and offers twenty pounds for 'such information as may lead . . . etc'. And even the Reform Committee, alarmed at the scale and momentum of protest, appeals to the inhabitants 'to abstain from these nightly tumultuous assemblages which have led to these breaches of the peace' [115]. (Although it does not bear Mr Shipp's imprint, there is reason to believe that this last also is a production by Mr

(page 30)

WHEREAS printed Papers have been posted up and distributed in various Parts of the Metropolis, advertizing that a Public Meeting will be held in *Cold Bath Fields*, on *Monday* next, *May* 13th, to adopt preparatory Measures for holding a National Convention, as the only Means of obtaining and securing the Rights of the People:

And whereas a Public Meeting holden for such a Purpose is dangerous to the Public Peace, and illegal:

All Classes of His Majesty's Subjects are hereby warned not to attend such Meeting, nor to take any Part in the Proceedings thereof.

And Notice is hereby given, That the Civil Authorities have strict Orders to maintain and secure the Public Peace, and to apprehend any Persons offending herein, that they may be dealt with according to Law.

By Order of the Secretary of State.

LONDON: Printed by GEORGE EYRE and ANDREW SPOTTISWOODE, Printers to the King's most Excellent Majesty. 1833.

EDINBURGH & GLASGOW
RAILWAY.
CAUTION.

JOHN WHITTON, Sailor, belonging to H.M. Ship "Jackall," Charged with being Drunk and Disorderly in the 2 p.m. Train from Edinburgh to Glasgow, on Saturday, the 4th July current, and with Annoying and Assaulting his fellow Passengers. He had to be taken from the Train at Falkirk Station, and was brought before Sheriff SCONCE, and Fined in the Sum of

5 Shillings,
Or Eight Days' Imprisonment.
COMPANY'S OFFICES,
GLASGOW. July. 1863.
BY ORDER.

M'CORQUODALE & CO., Printers, 85 Maxwell Street, Glasgow.

41 Glasgow 1863   **42** London 1833

LANCASTER & CARLISLE
RAILWAY.
CAUTION
to
TRESPASSERS.

On the 8th November 1851, James Cain, whilst trespassing on the Railway near South-waite Station, was struck down by a Train and killed on the spot.

The Company hereby give NOTICE of their intention to PROSECUTE all Trespassers under the powers of the Acts of Parliament.

BY ORDER.

A. MILNER, PRINTER, GUARDIAN OFFICE, CHURCH STREET, LANCASTER.

Stolen or Strayed,
FROM SUMMER-HILL,
NEAR ULVERSTON,

On or about the 5th Day of May, 1811,

An Iron-Gray Mare,
FOUR YEARS' OLD,

About 14 Hands high, shews a little blood, fired on the far Footlock joint, blistered on the hind Hough, Bob Tail, and without Shoes.

Any Person who will give Information of the said Mare, or bring her to Mr. *William Shuttleworth*, of *Summer-hill*, shall be HANDSOMELY REWARDED.

October 3d, 1811.

J. SOULBY, PRINTER, ULVERSTON.

43 Lancaster 1851   **44** Ulverston 1811

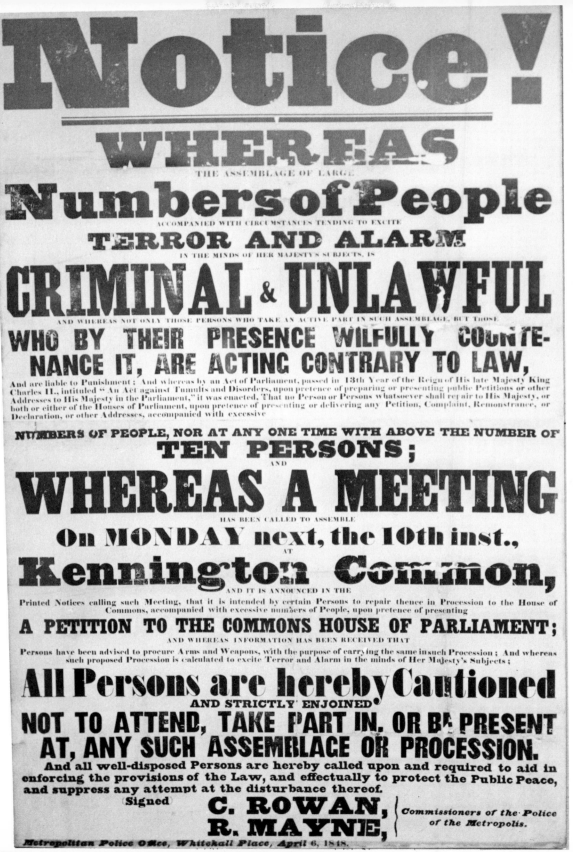

Notice!

WHEREAS

THE ASSEMBLAGE OF LARGE

Numbers of People

ACCOMPANIED WITH CIRCUMSTANCES TENDING TO EXCITE

TERROR AND ALARM

IN THE MINDS OF HER MAJESTY'S SUBJECTS, IS

CRIMINAL & UNLAWFUL

AND WHEREAS NOT ONLY THOSE PERSONS WHO TAKE AN ACTIVE PART IN SUCH ASSEMBLAGE, BUT THOSE

WHO BY THEIR PRESENCE WILFULLY COUNTE-NANCE IT, ARE ACTING CONTRARY TO LAW,

And are liable to Punishment; And whereas by an Act of Parliament, passed in 13th Year of the Reign of His late Majesty King Charles II., intituled "An Act against Tumults and Disorders, upon pretence of preparing or presenting public Petitions or other Addresses to His Majesty in the Parliament," it was enacted, That no Person or Persons whatsoever shall repair to His Majesty, or both or either of the Houses of Parliament, upon pretence of presenting or delivering any Petition, Complaint, Remonstrance, or Declaration, or other Addresses, accompanied with excessive

NUMBERS OF PEOPLE, NOR AT ANY ONE TIME WITH ABOVE THE NUMBER OF

TEN PERSONS;

AND

WHEREAS A MEETING

HAS BEEN CALLED TO ASSEMBLE

On MONDAY next, the 10th inst.,

AT

Kennington Common,

AND IT IS ANNOUNCED IN THE

Printed Notices calling such Meeting, that it is intended by certain Persons to repair thence in Procession to the House of Commons, accompanied with excessive numbers of People, upon pretence of presenting

A PETITION TO THE COMMONS HOUSE OF PARLIAMENT;

AND WHEREAS INFORMATION HAS BEEN RECEIVED THAT

Persons have been advised to procure Arms and Weapons, with the purpose of carrying the same in such Procession; And whereas such proposed Procession is calculated to excite Terror and Alarm in the minds of Her Majesty's Subjects;

All Persons are hereby Cautioned

AND STRICTLY ENJOINED

NOT TO ATTEND, TAKE PART IN, OR BE PRESENT AT, ANY SUCH ASSEMBLAGE OR PROCESSION.

And all well-disposed Persons are hereby called upon and required to aid in enforcing the provisions of the Law, and effectually to protect the Public Peace, and suppress any attempt at the disturbance thereof.

(Signed)

C. ROWAN,
R. MAYNE,
Commissioners of the Police of the Metropolis.

Metropolitan Police Office, Whitehall Place, April 6, 1848.

45
London
1848

29

REWARD.

WHEREAS, some wicked rude and evil minded Persons, or ill educated Boys, have been in the Practice of throwing Stones into a GARDEN situate at the head of *Dalton-gate*, opposite those Houses called *Backhouse's Buildings*, endangering the Lives of those walking therein. Certain it is that on Saturday the 10th Instant, a poor Woman following her daily Labour of Weeding, complained of nearly losing her Senses, by a violent Blow received from a Stone thrown over as above mentioned.

Therefore this is to give Notice,

That if any one will give *true* Information to Mrs. DOCTOR FELL, the Owner of the said Garden, who the People are that do the Mischief, so that he, or they, may receive condign Punishment, such Person, effectually so doing, shall be

Handsomely Rewarded.

ULVERSTONE, September 12th, 1808.

J. Soulby, PRINTER, Ulverston.

TEN GUINEAS' REWARD.

WHEREAS many of the Inhabitants of the Parish of CARTMEL have, for some Time past, suffered by various Articles being stolen from about their Premises, and wanton Mischiefs done to their Gates and Fences; particularly Mr. JOHN GARDNER and others in CARTMEL have had the Keys taken from their Doors, Poultry from their Yards, and Fruit from their Orchards; and Mr. NICHOLAS HARRISON and others about FLOOKBURGH have had Hay, Straw, Grain, Work Tools, and various Articles taken away:

Notice is hereby given

that A REWARD OF TEN GUINEAS will be given to any Person who will give such Information to the *Committee of the CARTMEL ASSOCIATION*, as may be the Means of convicting any such Offenders, to be paid by

John Gardner, ⎫
Robert Galloway, ⎬ Cartmel
Joseph Dixon, Cark
John Rawlinson, Greenbank
John Atkinson, Broughton

the Committee for the present Year, 1810.

J. SOULBY, Printer, ULVERSTON.

Shipp, who may by this time be feeling more than a printer's interest in these matters.)

The years of the Reform agitation were by no means the only period of riot, incendiarism and public notices. For over half a century the people of Dorset lived with unrest. In January 1817 a notice appeared in Piddletown (a village later to become famous for its associations with the Tolpuddle Martyrs). It said, *If Wages is not ris'd and Burt murdered or discharged from the Generels, Piddletown shall soon be in flames, so help us God.* The notice was quoted verbatim in another notice, this time published by a group of gentry – among them the Earl of Orford, two generals and Burt himself. Fifty guineas was offered for the 'bringing to justice of the offenders'. Already the threat of incendiarism was an offence as serious as incendiarism itself.

In 1820 more trouble threatened, this time over a subject which had become scarcely less inflammatory, the morals of Her Majesty the Queen. Queen Caroline's trial for adultery had divided opinion in Dorset as it had done throughout the country. When the charges against her were dropped there were many who sought to celebrate by illuminating their houses. There were also many who sought no such celebration.

A notice duly appeared, signed by some two dozen citizens. Signatories included not only Simmonds, the printer of the notice, but one of the Shipp brothers, his competitors. Strength of feeling had transcended even commercial differences. The notice said that whereas certain Blandford inhabitants intended to illuminate their houses, the signatories (most of whom declared themselves as special constables) would regard any such illumination as a potential breach of the peace. The full text [175] left the illuminators in no doubt of their position if they should proceed with their intention.

The illuminating of houses as a mark of celebration was a matter of continual friction. At any impending jubilation, notices invariably appeared *for* and *against*. When the Reform Bill was finally passed in 1832 there was the usual urgent flurry of printed declarations. One such announcement survives in which the publisher, though defiantly declaring his intention to illuminate, by design or accident remains anonymous.

At one level or another discord and unrest continue as a theme in the specimen books of the Dorset printers. In 1850 Mr Shipp records again the presence of fire-raisers [18], and in 1859 a notice printed by Mr Bartlett inveighs against the Church of England *(page 38)*

A BOY LOST.

LONDON, NOVEMBER 10, 1796.

LOST Yesterday, (Lord Mayor's Day, between Four and Five o'Clock in the Afternoon, a Boy, between Twelve and Thirteen Years old, of a fair, pale Complexion, roundish Face, and Hair rather light and short, his Shirt was open at the Neck, and had on a Black Coat, Scarlet Waistcoat, corded Thickset Breeches, White Stockings, and Half Boots laced before; was much dirtied, in consequence of having gone to see the Lord Mayor's Shew.

Whoever will bring him to his distressed Mother, *Mary Fenner*, at No. 17, *Mitre Court Buildings, in the Temple*, or will give her Information respecting him, will be gratefully thanked, and rewarded for their Trouble.

** *He need not be afraid of returning Home.*

48
London
1796

31

BOROUGH OF DORCHESTER.

The MAYOR having received a Circular Letter from The Right Hon. The LORD MAYOR OF LONDON, requesting his co-operation in aid of the Funds now collecting in the Metropolis, to mitigate the SUFFERINGS AND IMMEDIATE WANTS of the distressed SPANISH and ITALIAN REFUGEES still remaining in this Country, hereby informs the Inhabitants that Books are opened for Subscriptions on behalf of those unfortunate Strangers, at the several BANKS and LIBRARIES in the Town.

By Order of the Mayor,

J. STONE,
Town-Clerk.

Dated 19th December, 1828.

G. CLARK, PRINTER, CORNHILL, DORCHESTER.

49 Dorchester 1828

Public Office, Bow Street.

JUNE 4, 1806.

MISSING.

WHEREAS a YOUNG MAN left his Employer's House in the Neighbourhood of SLOANE STREET, on Sunday laſt, for the Purpoſe of viſiting ſome Friends, and not having returned ſince, great Fear is entertained for his Safety. He was with ſome other young Men at Bagnigge Wells that Afternoon, and parted with them near the Turnpike, Spa Fields, about Half paſt Nine the ſame Evening.

Whoever will give any Information at the above Office, that may lead to his being diſcovered, ſhall receive *FIVE GUINEA*S Reward from his Employer.

Said Young Man is about 21 Years of Age, 5 Feet 8 Inches high, florid Complexion, light Eyes, light-brown Hair, cropped, rather large Noſe, and has loſt the firſt Joint of one Finger; was dreſſed in a black Coat, white Dimity Waiſtcoat, drab Kerſeymere Breeches, white Cotton Stockings, and Shoes tied; is of very reſpectable Appearance.

J. Downes, Printer, Strand, London.

50 London 1806

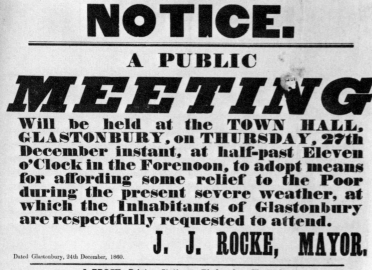

51 Glastonbury 1860

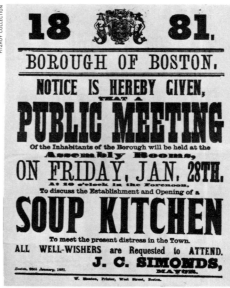

52 Boston, Lincolnshire 1881

FEVER HOSPITAL IN ISLINGTON.

A PUBLIC MEETING

OF THE

INHABITANTS OF ISLINGTON

WILL TAKE PLACE

This Evening, FRIDAY, JUNE 4th, 1847,

AT THE

FOX TAVERN, ISLINGTON GREEN,

At Seven o'Clock precisely,

To adopt measures to oppose the introduction of a Fever Hospital in this Parish, which if carried into effect, will deteriorate the value of property, and be injurious to the health of the Inhabitants in the neighbourhood.

T. WAKLEY & T. S. DUNCOMBE, Esqrs.

Members for the Borough of Finsbury, are expected to attend.

J. LITTON PRINTER, ISLINGTON.

3 Islington 1847

SAINT GEORGE in the EAST.

CHILD FOUND

Where	Cable-street, St. George in the East
When	28th June, 1875.
Sex	Female.
Name (if known)	Not known.
Apparent age	3 years.
Complexion	Fair.
Hair (colour of)	Light Brown.
Particular marks on the person	None.
Dress, and marks thereon	Hat trimmed with Velvet, Brown Stuff dress, Black cloth jacket, Grey cotton flannel petticoat, lace-up boots, Red and Black striped scarf, marked " M. J."
Any statement made by the child as to his or her abode ?	None.

NOW in the WORKHOUSE,

Charles-street, Old Gravel-lane,

ST. GEORGE IN THE EAST.

Dated this 3rd day of July, 1875.

54 London 1875

COUNTY BOROUGH OF OLDHAM.

SWINE FEVER

(INFECTED AREAS.)

BY THE BOARD OF AGRICULTURE.

THE Board of Agriculture by virtue and in exercise of the powers in them vested under the Board of Agriculture Act, 1889, and the Contagious Diseases (Animals) Acts, 1878 to 1893, and of every other power enabling them in this behalf, do order, and it is hereby ordered as follows:

1. Each of the Areas described in the Schedule to this Order is hereby declared to be an Area infected with swine-fever for the purposes of the Swine-Fever (Infected Areas) Order of 1894, dated the twenty-sixth day of January, one thousand eight hundred and ninety-four.

2. This Order shall take effect from and immediately after the eighteenth day of February, one thousand eight hundred and ninety-four.

In witness whereof the Board of Agriculture have hereunto set their Official Seal this sixth day of February, one thousand eight hundred and ninety-four.

T. H. ELLIOTT,
SECRETARY

SCHEDULE.

(5.) An Area comprising the County of Lancaster (except the Hundred of Lonsdale North of the Sands), and also comprising the Boroughs of Accrington, Ashton-under-Lyne, Bacup, Blackburn, Blackpool, Bolton, Bootle, Burnley, Bury, Chorley, Clitheroe, Darwen, Eccles, Haslingden, Heywood, Lancaster, Liverpool, Manchester, Middleton, Mossley, Nelson, OLDHAM, Preston, Rawtenstall, Rochdale, St. Helens, Salford, Southport, Warrington, Widnes & Wigan.

Published by the Local Authority pursuant to Section 192 of the Animals Order of 1886.

A. NICHOLSON,

TOWN CLERK.

Town Hall, Oldham, February 9th, 1894.

THOS. DORNAN, PRINTER, &c., 99, UNION STREET, OLDHAM.

55 Oldham 1894

33

IMBECILE
WARD KEEPERS
WANTED.

The Guardians of Mile End Old Town require the services of a **MALE** and **FEMALE**, to take charge of the **HARMLESS LUNATICS** in the Workhouse Infirmary. Candidates must be active, healthy, patient, without encumbrance, and between twenty-five and fifty years of age.

SALARY } **MALE - - £25.**
FEMALE - £20.

With Board, Lodging, and Washing,
A MAN AND WIFE PREFERRED.

Applications in the Candidate's own hand-writing, marked on the outside "M" or "F," as the case may be, stating age, and where previously employed, accompanied by **THREE TESTIMONIALS**, of recent date, must reach me before Twelve o'Clock on **THURSDAY**, 19th instant, on which day at Three, applicants must attend at their own expense. A selection will then be made, and the appointment take place at Six in the Evening, of the said 19th. No one need apply whose character for honesty, sobriety, and competency, will not bear the strictest investigation.
Canvassing the Guardians is prohibited.

(By Order,)

E. J. SOUTHWELL,
Clerk.

Workhouse, Bancroft Road, Stepney, N.E.
7th December, 1861

56
Lor
186

T. PENNY, PRINTER, 121, LEMAN STREET, WHITECHAPEL.

MILE END OLD TOWN.

DESERTION

ONE GUINEA
REWARD.

𝕎𝕙𝕖𝕣𝕖𝕒𝕤,

REUBEN EDWARDS

Formerly of Charles Street, Stepney, COWKEEPER, afterwards Laborer, of Wade's Place, Mile End Road, did, in the month of May last, run away and leave his Wife Frances, aged 41, and their Two Children, Mary Hannah, aged 8 years, and Jane, aged 6 years, in a state of destitution, and whereby they have become, and are now, inmates of the Workhouse of, and chargeable to, the Hamlet of Mile End Old Town. The said Reuben Edwards is 37 years of age, 5ft. 6in. high, thick set, of very dark complexion, and has full whiskers, generally dresses in corduroy trowsers, and a smock frock.

He is supposed to be in the neighbourhood of Bethnal Green or Sydenham.

Any person giving such information as will lead to the apprehension and conviction of the said Reuben Edwards, shall receive the above Reward.

(By Order of the Board of Guardians),

E. J. SOUTHWELL, Clerk.

Workhouse, Bancroft Road, N.E.,
29th November, 1861.

57
London
1861

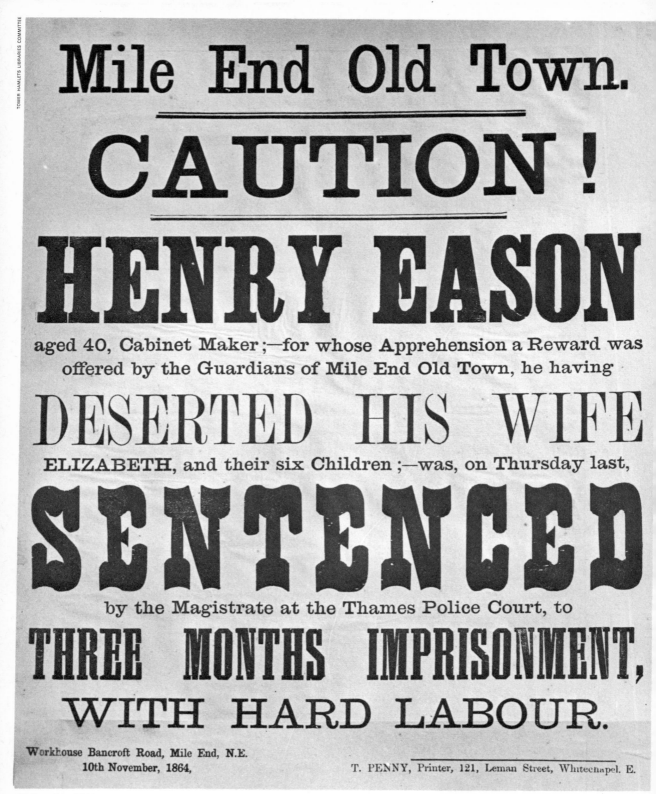

Mile End Old Town.

CAUTION !

HENRY EASON

aged 40, Cabinet Maker;—for whose Apprehension a Reward was offered by the Guardians of Mile End Old Town, he having

DESERTED HIS WIFE

ELIZABETH, and their six Children;—was, on Thursday last,

SENTENCED

by the Magistrate at the Thames Police Court, to

THREE MONTHS IMPRISONMENT,

WITH HARD LABOUR.

Workhouse Bancroft Road, Mile End, N.E.
10th November, 1864,

T. PENNY, Printer, 121, Leman Street, Whitechapel. E.

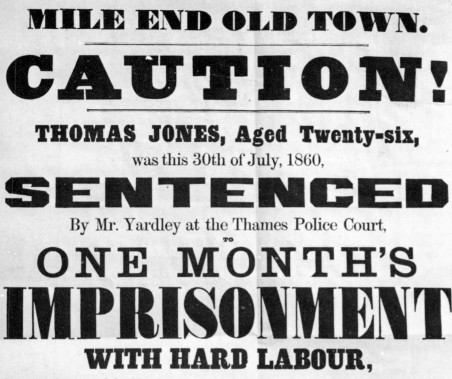

MILE END OLD TOWN.

CAUTION!

THOMAS JONES, Aged Twenty-six,

was this 30th of July, 1860,

SENTENCED

By Mr. Yardley at the Thames Police Court,

TO

ONE MONTH'S
IMPRISONMENT

WITH HARD LABOUR,

for tearing up his Clothes in the Casual Ward of this Workhouse.

London 1860

BOROUGH OF
Blandford Forum.

Having received a requisition of which the following is a Copy,

"To the Bailiff of
BLANDFORD,

WE the undersigned Inhabitants of this Parish regarding with serious alarm the reports of the CHOLERA having reached this Country, respectfully request you to call a Meeting of the Inhabitants at your earliest convenience, to take into consideration the adoption of such precautionary measures as the urgency of the Case may require,

Signed,

G. W. I. CHARD, Vicar.	JOHN DURDEN.
W. C. HEYWOOD.	HENRY W. JOHNS.
THOMAS WISE.	W. S. STRADLING.
JOHN DANSEY.	W. HENVILLE.
M. FISHER.	JOHN BARFOOT.
JOHN WHITE.	WILLIAM HOWSE.
WILLIAM ROE	HENRY ABBOTT.
JOHN SHIPP, Jun.	W. TATCHELL.
ROBERT BASKETT.	A. HODGES.

Blandford, November 9th, 1831."

I do in compliance therewith convene a Meeting of the Inhabitants of this Borough and Town, to be held at the TOWN-HALL, on *Friday, the 11th of November inst.* at the Hour of 10 in the Morning, for the purposes in such Requisition mentioned.

SEPTIMUS SMITH, *Bailiff.*

Blandford, 10th November, 1831.

Shipp, Printer, Blandford.

62 Blandford 1831

BLANDFORD.
INDIAN FAMINE
Relief Fund.

The Lord Mayor of London, in pursuance of a Resolution passed at a Public Meeting at the Mansion House, having invited the Co-operation of the LOCAL AUTHORITIES throughout the United Kingdom in AID of the above FUND, I beg leave to inform the Inhabitants of the Town and Neighbourhood of BLANDFORD, that

SUBSCRIPTION LISTS

Have been opened at the several

Banking Establishments

within the Borough, where Contributions will be received, and be duly forwarded to the London Committee.

THOMAS H. BENNETT,
MAYOR.

Blandford, April 29th, 1861.

W. SHIPP, PRINTER BLANDFORD.

Blandford 1861

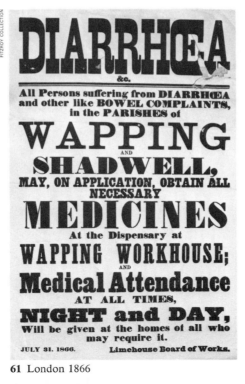

DIARRHŒA
&c.

All Persons suffering from DIARRHŒA and other like BOWEL COMPLAINTS, in the PARISHES of

WAPPING
AND
SHADWELL,

MAY, ON APPLICATION, OBTAIN ALL
NECESSARY

MEDICINES

At the Dispensary at

WAPPING WORKHOUSE;
AND

Medical Attendance
AT ALL TIMES,

NIGHT and DAY,

Will be given at the homes of all who may require it.

JULY 31. 1866. **Limehouse Board of Works.**

61 London 1866

BOROUGH OF
BLANDFORD.

AT a Meeting of the Inhabitants of the Borough and Town of Blandford Forum, held at the TOWN-HALL, on Friday, the 11th Day of November, 1831, convened by the Bailiff, pursuant to a requisition from many of the Inhabitants, for the purpose of taking into consideration the adoption of precautionary measures against the introduction of the CHOLERA, in consequence of the reports that it has reached this Country being confirmed.

THE BAILIFF IN THE CHAIR.

I. It was proposed by the *Rev. R. Keynes,* and seconded by *W. C. Heywood, M. D.* and by the Meeting unanimously resolved, that a **Board of Health** be established in this Town, with full powers to adopt all such measures as may appear to be necessary.

II. It was proposed by *W. C. Heywood, M. D.* and seconded by the *Rev. G.W.I. Chard,* and unanimously agreed, that the Board consist of the following persons, viz:— *The Bailiff, the Medical Gentlemen of the Town, the Rev. G. W. I. Chard, Vicar, Rev. J. P. McGhie, Rev. R. Keynes, Rev. Dr Wise, Mr. Dansey, Sen. Colonel Churchand, Mr. W. Fisher, Capt. Brine, Mr. J. Brine,* and *Mr. G. Stuart,* with power to add to their number.

III. It was proposed by *Mr. Daniell,* and seconded by *Mr. E. O. Spooner,* and agreed unanimously, that a Committee be appointed to assist the Board, and that such Committee consist of the following names, viz:—*The Churchwardens, the Visitor, and Overseers, the Waywardens, Mr. M. Fisher, Mr. Durden, Mr. W. Roe, Mr. Harrison, Mr. Johns, Mr. Simmonds, and Mr. Barnes, Jun.* and that such Committee be authorised to add to their number.

IV. Resolved that these Resolutions be printed and circulated in the Town.

V. Resolved that these Resolutions be signed on the behalf of the Meeting by the Chairman.

SEPTIMUS SMITH, *Bailiff.*

Resolved unanimously that the thanks of this Meeting be given to the Bailiff for his readiness in calling the same, and for his conduct in the Chair.

Blandford, 11th November, 1831.

Shipp, Printer, Blandford.

63 Blandford 1831

as an expropriator of farm-carts [132]. Blandford was not the only centre of unrest. Nor was it the only area in which reformers were themselves obliged to sound a note of restraint to their followers. Cullompton's appeal for moderation in 1847 [90] echoes that of Blandford in 1831 [115]. The fires that had started at the Bastille in 1789 had spread far, and were a long time dying.

Vagrants or impostors?

Poverty is the real theme of the nineteenth-century notice. In Dorset as elsewhere, the Establishment began to be increasingly aware of the duality of its interest. It had always recognized the need to protect the haves from the have-nots; now it began to see the growing need to mitigate the lot of the have-nots.

But protection long remained uppermost. All over Britain there came into being Protection (or 'Prosecution') Societies, associations of property owners who sought to pool their resources in the fight against the intruder. They employed private foot-patrols, shared litigation and reward costs, and also shared printing costs for reward notices. Their announcements refer to a wide range of larceny: valuable silver in Dorchester [13], oddments in Ulverston [47], cart-horse hair in Horsham [22] and an 18-gallon wash-house copper from Lewes [25].

Among their main concerns was the protection of game. As the law stood, wild life of any description was the property of those on whose land it flourished. More than that: the right to hunt was legally confined to a specific category – to those holding an estate to a yearly value of £100 or over. Only the elder sons of esquires, and persons above that rank, were allowed to shoot at all; no other person was allowed to deal in game in any way, whether by buying and selling it, or by carrying it and storing it. To consume game, except by invitation of the landlord, was an offence.

Warning notices of the period reflect the law. The Ulverston 'Game' notice [86], distinguishing between a polite request to 'Gentlemen Sportsmen' and a warning of prosecution to 'all other persons' expresses not only a social nicety but a legal one.

The law was severe. An Act of 1817 laid it down that any unauthorized person found in any forest, chase or park with an offensive weapon was to be tried at Quarter Sessions, and, if convicted, to be sentenced to transportation for seven years. If the offender returned to Britain during that period, it added, he was to be transported for life. Effectively,

either sentence amounted to life banishment; the poverty level of offenders was a bar to anything much in the way of return travel.

In conditions of increasing poverty, and with often only a hedge or a fence – sometimes only an invisible boundary line – separating a hungry family from a square meal, the Game Laws were widely ignored. Poaching became a major popular activity. In the three years between 1827 and 1830 official records quote one in seven of all convictions in Britain as convictions under the Game Code.

So wholehearted and so universal was contempt for the law that gamekeeping moved into a mechanized phase. Landlords took to defending their property with hidden weapons – many of them uncompromisingly lethal.

Man-traps, spring guns and other devices were installed by the score. Sydney Smith described the country as 'a whole land filled with lurking engines of death – machinations against human life under every green tree'.

In psychological support of these devices was the printed warning. Often this was the chief deterrent; often in fact it was displayed where no device was present. Before long the wording descended to a frank expression of a war of nerves [85].

The notice had a dual function. The landlord viewed it not only as a deterrent but, in cases where victims might claim compensation for injury, as a form of defence in law. It was held – although the point was not at the time finally settled as a principle – that due warning absolved the landlord from responsibility.

Whatever its rationale, the man-trap notice proliferated. Soon, by its very numbers, it lost credibility. Increasingly those who ignored it, innocent and guilty alike, paid for their growing boldness with injury and death.

Even as the battle with a poaching populace intensified, the role of the Protection and Prosecution interests began in some areas to change. However valid the man-trap and spring gun, the tide of poverty could no longer be entirely ignored. In towns and villages everywhere, vagrancy, begging and petty crime became more than a mere nuisance.

Confused by the narrowness of the margins that separated the pauper from the criminal, and seeking a means of averting a threatening confrontation, the Establishment took steps. 'Relief' organizations came into being. These, immediate offspring of the Prosecution Societies, were designed to offer alms with one hand and punishment with the other.

Typical are the Blandford and Dorchester announcements of the formation of a 'Society for the Relief of Distressed Travellers and the Detection of Vagrants and Imposters' and a 'Society for the Suppression of Mendicity' [73, 75]. Here, in the fusion of the functions of relief and punishment, is the dichotomous face of Public Authority – a tweedledum and tweedledee concept that is not unfamiliar in the twentieth century.

In the Anglo-Saxon world, responsibility for the maintenance of Law and Order has historically rested with the people. The principle is in direct contrast to that of much of the rest of the world, where the civil police operation is seen as a side-line of the central military power.

'Keeping the King's Peace' – the basic Anglo-Saxon concept – was the collective responsibility of everybody in a given locality. It stemmed from an earlier proposition – that whole families, clans and neighbourhood groups were liable to punishment for the misdeeds of any one of their number. It had the effect of making each citizen his neighbour's keeper – an acting unpaid law-enforcement officer.

The principle still operates today: it is not merely the right, but the duty of a citizen to assist a police officer in apprehending a criminal; similarly if he sees a crime committed, or apparently about to be committed, it is his duty to make every effort to arrest the criminal himself.

The concept of 'the posse'

The notion of collective responsibility is expressed in the time-honoured *posse comitatus*, 'the power of the county'. The 'posse' was a well-known feature of the American West, and is still in many states of America a legally recognized civil instrument. It represents a reinforcement of the powers of the sheriff by the citizens themselves. (The word 'arrest', as it appears in reward notices addressed to the public, is used in a strictly specific sense; Sheriff Hogan's 1853 announcement [9], notwithstanding the illegality of its pre-judgement of the guilt of the fugitive, relies for its imperative on the Law.)

The idea of collective aid is classically present in the common-law 'Hue and Cry'. In this the constable or sheriff raises a general alarm and orders all able-bodied citizens, on pain of fine or imprisonment, to pursue the criminal. The practice dates back to earliest times: at one period the community was liable to punishment not only for failure to pursue but, having pursued, for failure to capture.

Hue and Cry was an instrument of very rough justice. In the hysteria that it invariably generated, the fugitive stood little chance; if he gave himself up he was deemed to be guilty; if he was overtaken on the run his captors were legally absolved from responsibility for the injuries he inevitably suffered. In Britain the practice was abolished by statute in 1827, but in America it survived in one form or another for many years. The expression 'Dead or Alive', by-word of the 'Wanted' notice in the West [30], stemmed directly from the concept of Hue and Cry. It went a stage further. It was not merely an implicit exoneration of any possible killing of the fugitive, it was a specific invitation to kill him.

Law and Order in the American West was a procedurally simple matter: in one well-known printed notice, published in Las Vegas in 1881, 'thieves, thugs, fakirs, bunko-steerers'* and others are warned that if they are found within the limits of the city after sunset they will be 'invited to a grand neck-tie party, the expense of which will be borne by 100 Substantial Citizens'. Lynch law, another close relation of Hue and Cry, has also been a long time dying.

Throughout history, the guardian of the peace on his own has had a rough time of it. Whether by summary command, or by formal short-term appointment, the recruiting of popular support has been a continuing necessity.

Certainly, in the earliest stages, the guardian of the peace needed more help than he was ever likely to get. His own resources were minimal. The eighteenth-century 'watchman', typical of his time, inspired no one's support.

Unwilling successor to a long and ineffectual line of 'tything-men', 'headboroughs' and beadles, the watchman was a liability at the best of times. Patrick Colquhoun, magistrate and reformer of the 1780s and 90s, described him as 'aged . . . and often feeble' and, because of his pitifully low wages, 'almost on every occasion half-starved'. Often the man was appointed from motives of humanity – simply as a means of giving an unemployable old man a job and keeping him out of the workhouse.

Old and feeble as they were, many such men found no difficulty in accepting gifts from their lawful prey. 'Money is received from disorderly persons in the night, to permit them to escape from the just punishment of the laws,' said Colquhoun. At best, the watchman was a sleepy old fool; at worst, he was a focal point of lawlessness.

By the end of the eighteenth century, crime rates

* *Fakirs: swindlers; bunko-steerers: confidence-tricksters.*

were rising rapidly; an uncoordinated pattern of beadles, watchmen, supervisors and local constables [5] had wholly failed to stem the tide.

Reinforcement, historically a matter of calling for 'Special Constables' or bringing in the military, was clearly not a long-term remedy. What was needed was a re-think of the entire police function.

In 1819, after soldiers had been called in to quell riots over Queen Caroline's return to England, the men mutinied; their action was in turn quelled by a detachment of the Life Guards. One result of the episode was a memorandum from the Duke of Wellington in which he said that the Government ought 'without the loss of a moment's time, to adopt measures to form either a police in London or a military corps which should be of a different description from the regular military force, or both'.

In 1829 Robert Peel's Metropolitan Police Act, embodying 'a New System of Police', came into being. The force, consisting of some three thousand men, was openly mistrusted by the public. In spite of its declaredly civilian status, the fact that it was uniformed, that it observed paramilitary discipline (and not least that it had been mooted by the Duke of Wellington) set popular opinion firmly against it: here, only thinly disguised, was a continental-style branch of the military; it must be resisted.

A major showdown was the clash at Cold Bath Fields in 1833. In April of that year printed notices appeared in London. Posted by the 'National Union of the Working Classes', they called among other things for the abolition of the monarchy and the House of Lords, and for a public meeting 'to adopt preparatory measures for holding a National Convention, the only means of obtaining and securing the rights of the people'.

The wording of the announcement was deemed to constitute an incitement to a breach of the peace. Within a few days another notice appeared [42]. This, bearing the royal crest, declared the meeting illegal and warned the public to keep away. Not for the first time, and certainly not for the last, notice and counter-notice declared open war.

When the day came, the meeting went ahead as planned. Some of the crowd had come armed with knives, and in the mêlée that developed two policemen were seriously injured and one was killed. On all counts it was an inauspicious first encounter.

In the controversy that followed, the official notice figured prominently: on the one hand its legality was questioned (there was doubt as to whether the Secretary of State had in fact formally authorized its publication); on the other it was widely held that the notice had served to give added publicity to an event which might otherwise have been largely ignored.

The matter of gratuitous publicity has exercised Authority on more than one occasion. Of the ten thousand people who attended the 'criminal and unlawful' Kennington Common meeting in 1848 [45], a fair proportion may have been brought there by the notice warning them to stay away. On the other hand it was argued that ten thousand was a poor showing against the half million the organizers had promised; it is possible that the Mayne and Rowan warning worked.

Although the 'New System of Police' had by the 1840s become an accepted instrument of the civil power, the Kennington Common affair evoked the old reactions: a force of 150,000 special constables was sworn in (among them one Louis-Napoleon, later to become emperor of France). As a final precaution the Government accepted the offer of the Duke of Wellington to look after the 'defence' arrangements. Quietly, on the night before the meeting, two or three pieces of cannon and a large number of soldiers were suitably deployed. Their presence, as it turned out, was not needed – nor was it afterwards formally disclosed.

Your neighbourhood father-figure

As the century unrolled, public confidence in the police increased. By the seventies and eighties the policeman was accepted not merely as an inevitable agency of control, but often as a welcome source of help and protection. Custodian of lost children, dispenser of information, colleague of fire- and ambulance-men, he moved perceptibly from bogeyman to father-figure.

The duality of roles is an echo of the eighteenth century. In point of fact, it dates from the earliest beginnings of local Watch and Ward: constables, beadles, supervisors, watchmen – though all were primarily concerned with crime prevention, all were also seen as custodians of the common good. They cried the hours and half-hours, cried also that 'all was well', and in their perambulations they watched not only for crime and 'disorderly and suspicious persons', but for unextinguished fires, defective street lamps, unauthorized refuse-tips, 'footpath and street nuisances' and other hazards. As the local authority combined relief with punishment, the constable combined welfare with control.

'Missing Person' notices put out under the heading *Public Office* epitomize the sharpening of the welfare focus: the 'Missing Young Man' notice [50], though pre-dating the inception of the New Police by over twenty years, is published from one of the seven London Police Offices (then known as Public Offices), forerunners of today's magistrates' courts. The office mentioned in the notice (a converted private house next door to an oyster warehouse) stood on a site close to that of the present Bow Street Police Station. The formal welfare role of the police began early.

It may be noted that the word 'police' itself had ambiguous beginnings. When the police idea was still a novelty, the word carried a connotation of 'general neighbourhood management'. When Colquhoun wrote his pioneering *Treatise of the Police of the Metropolis* he was setting out a view of the good order of the town; the word related as much to the proper regulation of civic affairs as to the prevention of crime. It was only by degrees that the word came to acquire its present-day sense.

On the one hand, it will be seen, crime control became tinged with welfare; on the other, in the workhouse, the poorhouse and the casual ward, welfare was tinged with punishment.

The tone and vocabulary of the typical workhouse notice reflects the area of confusion. The London notice with its disciplinary Rules and Orders [76] is not unrecognizably remote from the Australian prison notices [72, 74]; the sentence of one month's hard labour for the inmate who tore up his clothes in the Mile End Workhouse – together with its published cautionary warning [59] – is an indication of paternalism at its sharpest.

Poverty has long been equated with criminality. Homelessness, vagrancy, 'wandering abroad' and other evidences of instability have invited suspicion throughout history. In 1670, four years after the Great Fire of London, Charles II published a proclamation directed against those so depraved as to 'affect the destruction of His Majestie's said Royal City by fire' in the hopes of plunder and private gain. All 'Vagrant and Suspicious persons walking at unseasonable hours' were to be examined and searched for combustible matters, 'and in such case persons are not able to give a good account of themselves, they are forthwith to be conveyed before the next Justice of the Peace, to be proceeded against and severely punish'd according to the Law and the quality of their Offences'.

The whole history of relief is bound up with the 'threshold problem'. The homeless citizen, or vagrant, whose destitution defines him as a security risk, may be dealt with by moving him on to the next

district, by intermittently giving him enough sustenance to keep him out of trouble or by taking him in and looking after him. This last, in which the citizen broaches the threshold of Authority, is a delicate matter. Once having moved in, he is difficult to move out.

Behind many of the 'welfare' notices of the nineteenth century there lurks the fear of permanent encumbrance. Reuben Edwards [57] has left his wife and two children to be looked after. His capture is worth the printing and posting of a notice and one guinea reward. Henry Eason [58] has just failed to manage the same with a wife and six children; as a warning to others his fate is worth the publicity of a notice. The fate of Thomas Jones [59], incurred apparently in an effort to overstay his welcome in the casual ward, is also worth the trouble and expense of advertising. To the workhouse of the parish of St George in the East, the finding of a lost child – no rare happening – is not an unmixed blessing; to speed the matter of the child's disposal, and to ease the burden of repeated literary composition, a ready-printed questionnaire is overprinted with details as required [54].

In each of these cases Authority seeks to beat the threshold effect. The principle also appears in the community at large; though stirred to compassion for victims of disaster (and often more readily if they be distant strangers [60]), the private citizen is as wary as Authority in the matter of possible encumbrances. The anti-Fever Hospital notice that appeared in Islington in 1847 [53] is an unusually open expression of this; as with communities throughout history, fear of contamination – and particularly fear of the contaminated squatter – outweighs the call of charity.

Dirt, disease, disaster

Least popular of the contaminants, and least susceptible of control by the threshold principle, is cholera. Reaching Moscow from India and Afghanistan in the spring of 1830, cholera appeared in Europe in the following year and by the early months of 1832 had crossed the Atlantic to Quebec, New York and wide areas of North America. The United States had further epidemics in 1848, 1854, 1865 and 1873. Britain had four major outbreaks: in 1832, 1849, 1853 and 1865.

By the 1860s, though still imperfectly understood, the disease had been seen to be closely linked with the presence of dirt. The 'sanitarians', a lobby of gathering influence, though unable to pinpoint its

(*page 46*) 41

BOARD OF WORKS
FOR THE LIMEHOUSE DISTRICT.
COMPRISING LIMEHOUSE, RATCLIFF, SHADWELL & WAPPING.

In consequence of the appearance of **CHOLERA** within this District, the Board have appointed the under-mentioned Medical Gentlemen who will give ADVICE, MEDICINE, AND ASSISTANCE, FREE OF ANY CHARGE, AND UPON APPLICATION, AT ANY HOUR OF THE DAY OR NIGHT.

The Inhabitants are earnestly requested not to neglect the first symptoms of the appearance of Disease, (which in its early stage is easy to cure), but to apply, WITHOUT DELAY, to one of the Medical Gentlemen appointed.

The Board have opened an Establishment for the reception of Patients, in a building at Green Bank, near Wapping Church, (formerly used as Wapping Workhouse), where all cases of Cholera and Diarrhœa will be received and placed under the care of a competent Resident Medical Practitioner, and proper Attendants.

THE FOLLOWING ARE THE MEDICAL GENTLEMEN TO BE APPLIED TO:--

Mr. ORTON,
56, White Horse Street.

Dr. NIGHTINGALL,
4. Commercial Terrace, Commercial Road, (near Limehouse Church.)

Mr. SCHROEDER,
53, Three Colt Street, Limehouse.

Mr. HARRIS,
5, York Terrace, Commercial Road, (opposite Stepney Railway Station.)

Mr. CAMBELL,
At Mr. GRAY's, Chemist, Old Road, opposite "The World's End."

Mr. LYNCH,
St. James's Terrace, Back Road, Shadwell.

Mr. HECKFORD,
At the Dispensary, Wapping Workhouse.

BY ORDER,

BOARD OFFICES, WHITE HORSE STREET,
26th July, 1866.

THOS. W. RATCLIFF,
Clerk to the Board.

42

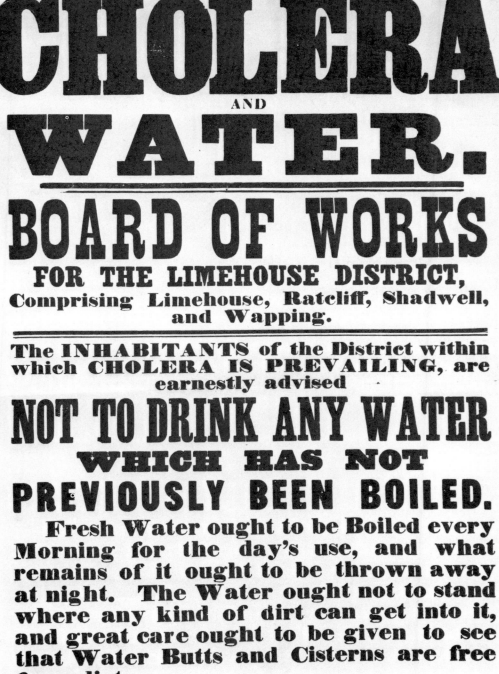

CHOLERA
AND
WATER.

BOARD OF WORKS

FOR THE LIMEHOUSE DISTRICT,
Comprising Limehouse, Ratcliff, Shadwell, and Wapping.

The **INHABITANTS** of the District within which **CHOLERA IS PREVAILING,** are earnestly advised

NOT TO DRINK ANY WATER
WHICH HAS NOT
PREVIOUSLY BEEN BOILED.

Fresh Water ought to be Boiled every Morning for the day's use, and what remains of it ought to be thrown away at night. The Water ought not to stand where any kind of dirt can get into it, and great care ought to be given to see that Water Butts and Cisterns are free from dirt.

BY ORDER,

THOS. W. RATCLIFF,
CLERK OF THE BOARD.

*Board Offices, White Horse Street,
1st August, 1866.*

43

65 London 1866

Proclamation !

In view of the great calamity that has befallen us, and for the better police and fire protection of the city, and for the better security of life and property, I hereby recommend that all the people remain at their homes during the coming night, from and after the hour of 7:30 p.m. of this day, and I do hereby command that all persons, save and except only those who have especial business to transact therein, and permission so to do, remain away from that part of the business section of the city now being especially patrolled.

ALL LAWLESSNESS WILL BE REPRESSED WITH A HEAVY HAND

The co-operation of all good citizens is invoked in aid of the enforcement of this Order.

G. D. WORSWICK
Mayor.

San Jose, Cal., April 18, 1906.

66 San José 1906

WARNING!

NOTICE IS GIVEN that any person found Pilfering, Stealing, Robbing, or committing any act of Lawless Violence will be summarily

HANGED

Vigilance Committee.

67 San Francisco 1906

PROCLAMATION
BY THE MAYOR

The Federal Troops, the members of the Regular Police Force and all Special Police Officers have been authorized by me to KILL any and all persons found engaged in Looting or in the Commission of Any Other Crime.

I have directed all the Gas and Electric Lighting Co.'s not to turn on Gas or Electricity until I order them to do so. You may therefore expect the city to remain in darkness for an indefinite time.

I request all citizens to remain at home from darkness until daylight every night until order is restored.

I WARN all Citizens of the danger of fire from Damaged or Destroyed Chimneys, Broken or Leaking Gas Pipes or Fixtures, or any like cause.

E. E. SCHMITZ, Mayor

Dated, April 18, 1906.

ALTVATER PRINT, MISSION AND 22D STS.

San Francisco 1906

GARBAGE

All householders and persons camping on Public squares or other places, are directed to remove all garbage and refuse from their premises to curb line of street for removal to crematory.

This rule must be observed in order to protect the health of the city.

DR. JAMES W. WARD
President Health Commission.

69 San Francisco 1906

Headquarters
Health Commission
TO THE PUBLIC

Food and Water Consumption

1. ALL WATER SHOULD BE BOILED, WHETHER FOR DRINKING, BATHING OR CLEANSING PURPOSES.

USE NO UNBOILED WATER IN THE PREPARATION OF FOOD FOR COOKING OR BAKING.

USE UNBOILED WATER ONLY FOR FLUSHING PURPOSES.

THIS ORDER APPLIES TO ALL WATER, WHETHER SPRING VALLEY, LAKE OR WELL WATER.

2. ALL MILK SHOULD BE BOILED, WHETHER USED BY INFANTS OR ADULTS.

3. FOOD IN CANS SHOULD NOT BE ALLOWED TO STAND UNCOVERED, LEST IT BECOME TAINTED OR INFECTED.

4. DO NOT EAT UNCOOKED VEGETABLES.

5. ALL BUTCHER SHOPS AND BAKERIES SHOULD BE SCREENED.

6. ALL CANNED GOODS SHOULD BE COOKED.

BY ORDER OF
DR. JAMES M. WARD,
PRESIDENT HEALTH COMMISSION.
SIGNED,
DR. D. F. RAGAN,
HEALTH OFFICER.

San Francisco 1906

PROCLAMATION!

The preservation of the good order and peace of the city is hereby entrusted to Lieut. General P. H. Sheridan, U. S. Army.

The Police will act in conjunction with the Lieut. General in the preservation of the peace and quiet of the city, and the Superintendent of Police will consult with him to that end.

The intent hereof being to preserve the peace of the city, without interfering with the functions of the City Government.

Given under my hand this 11th day of October, 1871.

R. B. MASON, Mayor.

71 Chicago 1871

method of transmission, were able to show that the disease flourished in 'conditions of poor sanitation'. For most big cities the description applied to virtually the whole urban area.

There were, however, districts of special risk. In London, the low-lying areas near the Thames were notorious. In the Limehouse and Shadwell districts, where polluted Thames water was the cleanest available supply, and where flushing lavatories were virtually non-existent, problems of sanitation were increased by overcrowding.

In a report in 1857 the Assistant Commissioner of Police described conditions in the common lodging houses. At No 93 High Street, Shadwell, were premises large enough for 25 persons; 45 people lived there. At No 117 Cock Hill, Ratcliff, in a room having space for 5, 15 people were found 'in a most deplorable condition'. At No 31 Farmer Street, Shadwell, a house of 6 small rooms, 29 people were found – one of·them lying in a cupboard dying, another, covered by an old rug, dead.

Just across the river in Bermondsey, Henry Mayhew observed the supply of drinking water: 'In the bright light it appeared the colour of strong green tea . . . It was more like watery mud than muddy water . . . As we gazed . . . we saw a whole tier of doorless privies . . . common to men and women, built over it. We heard bucket after bucket of filth splash into it . . . And yet . . . we saw a child from one of the galleries opposite lower a tin can with a rope, to fill a large bucket that stood beside her.' In these conditions, warnings about boiling water and not letting it stand 'where any kind of dirt can get into it' [65] may have seemed somewhat beside the point.

Very much to the point, in a more spectacular danger area, is the San Francisco earthquake notice [68], posted among the ruins on the afternoon of the disaster. Here again the public notice makes its mark. Here again, in a major emergency, and with divisions between haves and have-nots blurred by common danger, the threshold principle lapses.

When the proclamation went up, earthquake losses were calculated at some 500 lives and $20,000,000 material damage. The fire, clearly foreseen – and, with all water supplies destroyed, virtually inevitable – was yet to take its full toll. Four days later the town was a smouldering ruin; damage was estimated at $400,000,000 and 250,000 people were homeless.

One remarkable thing about Mayor Schmitz's declaration was not so much its ruthlessness but its relative calm. Much of the printed matter that emerged in the immediate aftermath showed understandable signs of dislocation. (The *Mercury-Herald* of nearby San José, first news-sheet to appear after the shock, carried more front-page misprints than possibly any newspaper before or since.) But the Schmitz proclamation was typographically cool and collected.

So, equally surprisingly, was Mayor Worswick's San José proclamation, given the same day [66]. So was the notice put out by the San José 'Vigilance Committee' [67], a one-man organization named Mr Coykendall, who feared the worst. Failing to arouse support for the formation of his vigilantes, he had the notices printed at this own expense and posted them up himself.

The personal public notice

Historically, it is not only in disaster and emergency, nor only as threat or warning, that the 'local' notice appears. With increasing social amenity, and with the widening of local authority responsibility, the notice becomes more and more an instrument of Colquhoun's 'general neighbourhood management'.

'Watching and Lighting' [77, 79], hitherto viewed as a dual function of public security, begins to give way to the simpler concept of lighting as an amenity. The arrival of gas as an illuminant – and as a commercial product – while helping to clarify one point, confuses another: is the gas company a public utility, or a profit-making business? Pre-installation notices, with their air of municipal authority [81, 82] present an adroit mixture of public announcement and commercial promotion. The presence of the mayor at initial proceedings [78] does nothing to clear up the ambiguity.

In other areas there is no doubt about municipal responsibility; in the matter of the custody of harmless lunatics for example [56], the municipality is strictly on its own. As the century develops, Boards of Guardians and Inspectors of Nuisances proliferate. By the turn of the century [55] the local-authority industry is impregnably entrenched.

The Public Notice, a tool of Neighbourhood Management, is also a handy tool of neighbourhood argument. In the nineteenth century it features as often in the personal wrangle as in the general clash of public opinion. With laws of libel less punctilious than today's, local personalities felt free to fight their battles by printed declaration.

More often than not it was a one-sided contest, with the protestor making most of the running. Such, clearly, was the case in the Newcastle area in

(*page 51*)

RULES

FOR

PRISONERS,

SEPARATE PRISON.

~~~

355.—The Prisoners are cautioned against committing any of the undermentioned Offences, for which they will be liable to punishment, viz.—communicating or attempting to communicate with each other, whether by words or signs; reading aloud; singing or making any other noise whatever, except such as may be unavoidable in the performance of their labour; not rising when the first bell is rung; not keeping their persons, cells, and the various articles provided for their use at all times clean and neatly arranged; leaving their cells improperly dressed, or without their designating badges; not keeping their clothes in proper repair; not maintaining the proper interval from each other, as directed, when proceeding to or from the chapel or the exercise-yards; not behaving with due respect and decorum during divine service; not treating the officers of the establishment and all visitors with due respect; addressing any officer or constable, except for some necessary purpose; not immediately reporting any article in their possession becoming broken or damaged by accident or otherwise; having any unauthorised article whatever in their possession; using their copy or other books, or slates,

for any unauthorised purpose; unrolling their bedding before the bell has been rung for that purpose; not extinguishing their cell-lights and retiring to rest at the appointed signal; removing the lamps without permission; allowing their lights to be too high.

356.—Any prisoner wishing to see the Governor, the Comptroller-General, the Commandant, the Chaplain, Medical Officer, or the Schoolmaster, will intimate his desire to the officer on duty, with the purport of the request or complaint he desires to make.

357.—Any complaint respecting the *quantity* of food must be made *before* the article is taken into the cell.

358.—Any other complaint is to be made to the Commandant or the Officer in charge immediately after the cause of such may have arisen.

359.—A copy of these Rules to be suspended in each cell.

(Extracts from Port Arthur Approved Regulations.)

72 Port Arthur *c* 1850

Blandford, Dorset.

~~~~~

A proposed Society for the Relief of distressed Travellers, and the Detection of Vagrants, and Impostors.

A general Meeting of the Inhabitants of Blandford and its Vicinity, for the purpose of taking into consideration the establishment of a Society as above, will be held at the TOWN HALL *of Blandford, on Monday August 2nd. 1819.*

At ONE o'Clock.

HENRY WHITE, *Bailiff.*

73 Blandford 1819

MESS ROOM
REGULATIONS.

216. The Prisoners are cautioned against committing any of the undermentioned offences, for which they will be liable to punishment, viz :

217. Not observing the strictest silence and decorum. Not suspending their caps upon the racks provided for that purpose. Not standing up during Grace before and after Meals.

218. Not arranging their Mess Utensils according to the prescribed method after Meals. Making any slop on the tables. Not observing the utmost cleanliness, or throwing any of the refuse upon the floor. Scratching or defacing any part of the Dining Hall, or Furniture thereof. The Mess-men not remaining at their respective Tables until they have delivered over the Mess Utensils to the Officers on duty.

(Extracts from Port Arthur Approved Regulations.)

74 Port Arthur *c* 1850

SOCIETY

FOR THE

Suppression of Mendicity,

In the Town and Neighbourhood of Dorchester,

ESTABLISHED DECEMBER 13th, 1819.

THE Plan of the Institution is the issue of printed Tickets for distribution to Street Beggars, which Tickets refer them to the Office of the Society, where each case is fully investigated and registered, and such Persons as appear to be deserving, are immediately supplied with Food, &c. and the necessary means adopted for detecting and bringing Impostors to Justice.

The Public are earnestly requested to assist the endeavours of the Society by Subscriptions, or purchasing and distributing Tickets; and discontinuing altogether the present impolitic practice of INDISCRIMINATE ALMSGIVING,—which is not Charity.

It is not, however, to be implied that the abstaining from Almsgiving is of itself sufficient, as the want of Benevolence may be sheltered beneath the affectation of Policy, and the sordid may avail themselves of so specious a pretence to refuse attention to the applications of the distressed.

It is not desired that the public Benevolence should be limited, but that it should be more judiciously—more usefully exercised. Let investigation always precede Relief, and the circumstances of every Case be minutely examined;—Relief will then be given to distressed and deserving objects.

As Investigation, however, is a duty which many have not leisure to perform, they are entreated to distribute the Society's Tickets; neither on the one hand allowing the applications of Beggars to be altogether disregarded, nor on the other endeavouring to rid themselves of clamourous importunity, by contributing to perpetuate a practice pregnant with every moral and political Evil.

T. GOULD READ, Mayor.

Subscribers are intitled to Tickets gratuitously;—to other Persons they are sold in Parcels of Twelve, at the charge of one Shilling, on application to Mr. GEORGE NEWMAN, the Registering Clerk.

** Subscriptions are received at the Bank, and at both the Libraries in Dorchester.

G. Clark, Printer, Dorchester.

May 1st, 1816.

RULES AND ORDERS,

To be observed by the Poor in this House.

IT is ordered by the Churchwardens, Overseers and Committee, that all Paupers resident in this Workhouse, do attend to the respective Employments allotted them on the Ringing of the Bell, (Sickness, &c. excepted,) the following Hours being appointed for their attendance, viz. from the 25th Day of March, to the 29th Day of September, from Six o'Clock in the Morning, until Six in the Evening, and from the 29th Day of September, until the 25th Day of March, from Eight o'Clock in the Morning, until Dark in the Evening, the usual Hours of Refreshment excepted; and it is strictly desired, that every Person, on leaving off Work, do wash themselves clean, and retire to the different Wards allotted for them, in a decent, orderly and becoming manner, and abide by all such reasonable and lawful Rules, as the Master or Mistress shall deem proper for the better Regulation of the House.

It is further Ordered, That all Persons not conforming strictly to the above Rules, or who shall idle away their Time in the Hours appointed for Work, on satisfactory Complaint being made to the Churchwardens or Overseers, the Allowance of the Person offending shall be stopped, (Bread and Beer excepted,) and in case of repeated Complaint, the Allowance of such Person to be again stopped, with the addition of Confinement, and if that fails to produce submission, then the Person so offending, to be taken before a Magistrate, and dealt with according to Law.

Also, that if any Pauper be found disposing of his or her Wearing Apparel, or allowance of Provisions; or any Person or Persons coming to see any Pauper, under pretence of being related or otherwise, and such Person or Persons shall be found with any Provisions of the House, Wearing Apparel, &c. in his, her, or their Possession, the Person or Persons so offending, shall immediately be taken before a Magistrate, and dealt with according to Law.

Lastly, that all Persons visiting Paupers in this House, shall obtain a Pass, or Permission from the Master or Mistress before they leave the Premises; and in case the Master or Mistress shall neglect their Duty in this respect, on Complaint being made by any of the Overseers or Committee to the Churchwardens, the Master or Mistress, as the case may be, shall be ordered before such Committee, and dealt with by them as they shall see fit, according to the nature of the Charge against them.

} *Churchwardens.*

NOTICE.

THE Inhabitants of BLANDFORD, having at a Public Meeting expressed their opinion that it would be more desirable the expences of WATCHING and LIGHTING the Town during the remainder of the Winter should be paid by Voluntary Subscription. The Inspectors appointed under the Watching and Lighting Act, refrain for the present from making a Rate, that opportunity may be given to ascertain whether so desirable an object can be effected by Subscription.

BLANDFORD, December 9th, 1831.

SHIPP, PRINTER, BLANDFORD.

77 Blandford 1831

A MEETING

Of the Inhabitants of the
BOROUGH OF BERKELEY,
WILL BE HELD AT THE
BERKELEY ARMS HOTEL,
On TUESDAY Evening Next,
At Six o'Clock,

To consider the propriety and possibility of Lighting the Town with

GAS.

WILLIAM GAISFORD,
MAYOR.

Berkeley 21st January, 1854.

POVEY, PRINTER, BERKELEY.

78 Berkeley, Gloucestershire 1854

We the undersigned request the favor of your calling a Public Meeting at Blandford, on such day as may be most convenient to take into consideration the propriety of forming a Plan for Watching the Town of Blandford during the ensuing Winter.

George W. I. Chard	I. W. Smith
Henry White	E. B. Portman
T. & W. Roe	M. Fisher
Henry W. Johns	H. F. Fisher
Stephen Carpenter	R. Keynes
John Dansey	

To the Bailiff of the Borough of Blandford.

Blandford, September 18th, 1829.

In compliance with the foregoing requisition I hereby appoint a Meeting to be held at the Guildhall on Thursday the 23rd of September Instant, at 11 o'Clock, for the above purpose.

J. White, Bailiff

Blandford, September 19th, 1829.

SHIPP, PRINTER, BLANDFORD.

79 Blandford 1829

PUBLIC CAUTION.
Brentford Gas Company

WHEREAS

JOHN LEEDON and **GEORGE CHAMBERS** have been convicted of Breaking One of the Company's LAMPS, placed by the Side of the Road at *HAMMERSMITH*, and not having paid the Penalty awarded against them, were *committed to the HOUSE of CORRECTION for the Space of*

ONE MONTH!

The Company give this Notice, that Offenders may know the Punishment they are liable to.

By Order of the Board,

BRENTFORD,
14th April, 1823.
Printed by W. GLINDON, Rupert Street, Haymarket.

THOS. JULLION, Clerk.

80 Brentford 1823

1835, when Mr Bacon Grey [102, 103] gave in to the directors of the railway over the use of the new Steam Locomotives across his land. It may be observed that the directors prudently hold their fire on the residual issue of Sunday Railways. With the no-trains-on-the-Lord's-Day lobby in mind, they declare that the trains will not travel on Sundays 'for the present'.

In similar personal vein is the flurry of notices generated by omnibus rivalries in London in the early 1850s [104, 108, 110]. More pointed still, in the 1830s, is the attack on a landlord-magistrate [87] for alleged injustice to a tenant-defendant, and its contemporary, 'Vote against Ponsonby' [130] – possibly the least devious election slogan of all time.

Less personal, but hardly less agressive, the notice put out by the owners of the good ship *Devon's Glory* [106] is as fine an example of 'knocking copy' as the century produced. At first glance the announcement is unexceptional; a measured reading discloses pure vitriol.

The public apology – final crunch in the polemic of the public notice – is a well-recognized formula. The present selection contains only three examples, the Ulverston bottle-thrower [88], the Thames boat-hook men [99] and the Grimsby ironmonger [101], but the output of the period was in fact high. Infractions of every sort, from spreading malicious tales to unspecified insulting behaviour, were the subject of long and sometimes tortuous essays of apology. Many, like the present specimens, were signed with a cross. On most occasions the offender was required to pay for the printing and posting of the notice. Often, as a last indignity, the notice recorded the fact.

The street servant's Christmas reminder, an item unique in printed ephemera, was produced to forestall, rather than to punish, infraction. This at least was the avowed intention of notices delivered to householders before Christmas; their messages enjoined the potential donor of a Christmas gift not to be misled into giving to any but the rightful recipient. To make sure of avoiding error, the notices explained, the true beneficiaries would show a specific medal, token or other item to identify themselves. ('As there are Persons who go about with intent to Defraud us and Impose upon you, be so kind as not to give your Bounty to any person, but to those who can produce a Medal as aforesaid . . .')

The notices were put out by lamplighters, dustmen and street-cleaning 'scavengers'. They were

81 Blandford 1836

82 Blandford 1836

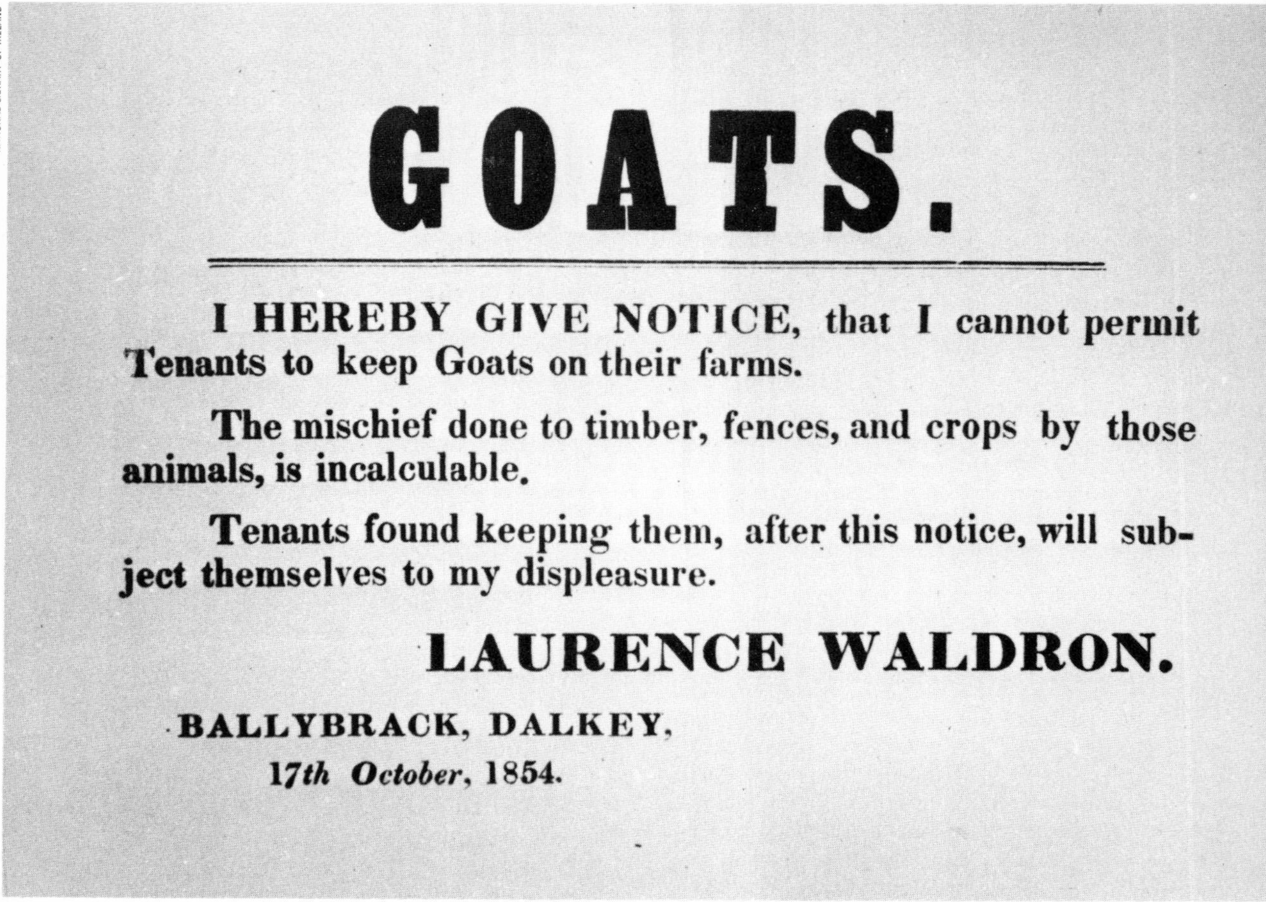

GOATS.

I HEREBY GIVE NOTICE, that I cannot permit Tenants to keep Goats on their farms.

The mischief done to timber, fences, and crops by those animals, is incalculable.

Tenants found keeping them, after this notice, will subject themselves to my displeasure.

LAURENCE WALDRON.

BALLYBRACK, DALKEY,
17th October, 1854.

83 Dalkey 1854

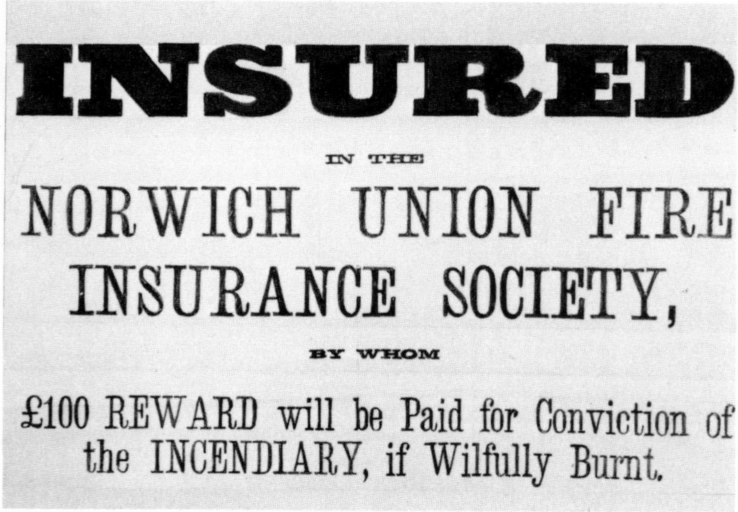

INSURED

IN THE

NORWICH UNION FIRE INSURANCE SOCIETY,

BY WHOM

£100 REWARD will be Paid for Conviction of the INCENDIARY, if Wilfully Burnt.

84 Norwich c 1832

GENTLEMEN
Tread Light!

Man Traps are set in These Grounds

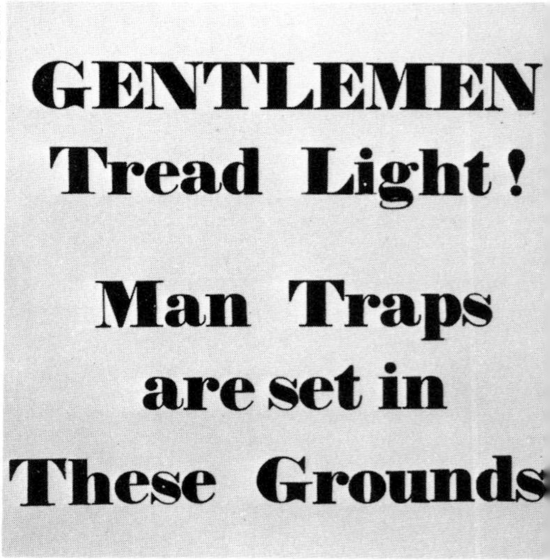

85 (?) c 1820

GAME.

Gentlemen Sportsmen

Are requested not to Hunt, Course
Shoot upon the Lands or Grounds
the Parish of Pennington, in the
ounty of Lancaster, belonging to or
the occupation of the Persons
hose names are hereunto subscri-
d:—All other Persons found tres-
ssing on such Lands or Grounds,
ill be prosecuted as the Law directs.

James Park	William Fleming
William Town	Isaac Dickinson
William Townson	Thomas Fell
Thomas Fisher	Iohn Huddleston

ston, September 20th 1825.

[J. Soulby, Printer, Market-place, Ulverston.]

86 Ulverston 1825

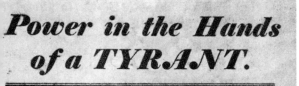

Power in the Hands of a TYRANT.

Who fined his Tenant renting
£1500. per Annum, 13l. 13s.
6d. for shooting a Moorhen?

Who was it? why Corfe Castle

BANKS!!

A most worthy Magistrate!!!

87 Wareham c 1830

separately produced for each of the districts concerned, and were also specific to the occupations in question: some, published by dustmen, carried the footline 'No connection with the scavengers'; others, from scavengers, said 'No connection with the dustmen'. Each, however, spoke darkly of interlopers; the lamplighters [178] went so far as to accuse their personators of actual disguise.

Even the Christmas Waits complained of sheep-stealers. The notice of Mrs Susanna Pole, widow of the Old-Established Wait of Saint Marylebone [176] advised that 'having to contend with opposition', she would call for her bounty in person, bringing with her the badge of office of her deceased husband.

The 'preliminary' notice was a commonly accepted convention, and survived in one form or another until the turn of the century. It echoed precisely the patent-medicine gambit, *None genuine without the maker's signature*.

A point for consideration is the florid literary style of these productions. As in a vast range of similar printed matter, the publishers affect a level of expression far outside their own colloquial range. It is true that many of their cadences are time-worn stereotypes. Mr Stephen Osborne, of the four-horse omnibus [108] makes use of a number of these – though he readily finds his own level on a more lively occasion [110].

High-flown phraseology appears generally in tradesmen's announcements throughout the century; it may be assumed that at an early stage somebody called in a copywriter. But less easy to explain is the resounding elegance of such *ad hoc* items as those of Susanna Pole and the scavengers and dustmen. That the tone is studiously genteel is not surprising, but the syntax is often remarkable. Whatever the defects of detail, the general construction, in convoluted reverberation and measured cadence, is impressive.

People for sale

As the printed notice spans the nineteenth century, its archives provide a continuous narrative. One ingredient in the narrative claims a big share of archive space. The Negro slave – for rent or for sale, dead or alive – is the century's major talking point.

It was in the United States that the issue finally reached flashpoint, and in Britain that the movement for abolition began, but it is to be recalled that Britain's trade in Negroes dates back to the time of Sir John Hawkins. Sir John's breaking of the Portuguese monopoly in the mid-1500s started a

SUBMISSION.

WHEREAS I RICHARD COUSEN, of *Bouth*, in *Lancashire*, Mariner, did on Thursday Evening the 20th of November Instant, throw a certain Glass Bottle out of the Gallery of the Theatre at *Ulverston*, to the imminent Danger of the Audience and Performers, for which Offence I have been apprehended and ordered to be prosecuted, but on account of my general good Character, at the Instance of Mr. BUTLER, the Manager, (whose Pardon and that of the Public at large I humbly solicit) I have been set at Liberty.

Now I do hereby promise never again to be guilty of any such Offence, and am very sorry for what I did, being in Liquor, and beg this Submission to be Printed and made Public as a Caution to all others, who may frequent the Theatre in future. As witness my Hand this 21st Day of November, 1806.

His

RICHARD † COUSEN.

Witness   JOHN THOMPSON, Constables.   Mark.
           RICHARD FELL,

...by, Printer. ...eet, Ulverston.

88 Ulverston 1806

DEFAMATION.

WHEREAS some evil disposed Person or Persons is employed in Circulating skandalous Reports injurious to the Character of Mrs. Tuck, No 6, Queen-street, Oxford-street. —who ever will give information of the Offender or Offenders, so that they may be brought to Justice, shall eb handsomely Rewarded for their trouble.

London April 9. 1816

Catnach Printer, Monmouth-court.

89 London 1816

54

business which was to become a key factor in Britain's national economy. Over the centuries the rounding up and shipping of African Negroes to the New World became a major invisible export. In the period 1680–1780 alone, the number of Negroes imported from Africa into the British colonies of America and the West Indies was well over two million. By 1790 one New York household in four owned one or more slaves.

Britain had her slaves too. Returning West Indian planters used them as domestic servants and bought and sold them through the 'small ad' columns of the British Press. By 1772, when a legal ruling declared them free men, the number of Negro slaves in the British Isles had reached 14,000.

With the trade in Africans a traffic as unremarkable as the buying and selling of cattle, it was not surprising that auction and sale notices appeared in the accepted terms of the market. The West Indies sale announcement [120] is typical; fourteen men and women appear on the same bill as a horse and a selection of household items. (Though the vendor's name does not appear in the notice, mention of the Government Printing Office in the footline suggests a person or persons of the highest respectability.)

As a variant to the outdoor sale, slaves were also offered as prizes in lotteries. On one such occasion a prize was 'the dark stout mulatto girl Sarah, aged about twenty years, general house servant, valued at nine hundred dollars, and guaranteed'. She served as second attraction in a bill featuring the main prize 'Star', a dark bay horse [119].

'Deliver him to the printer hereof . . .'

A perennial problem was the runaway slave. In public notices and in local newspapers, announcements regularly sought news of slave-owners' property. In tones reminiscent of the lost-dog appeal, worried advertisers offered substantial – if sometimes specialized – rewards: 'Run away from the subscriber on Saturday evening last a Negro boy named July, of the Chamba country. He is about 16 years of age, tall, rather lean . . . speaks very good English and had on when he went away, a check shirt with breeches. Any person who apprehends the said Negro, and will deliver him to the printer hereof, or to the subscriber at Port-Morant, shall receive Five pistoles, and all reasonable charges from John Kerr. N.B. As the Boy never ran away before, the subscriber is afraid he is forcibly detained by some person who, he hopes, on reading this will

(*page 65*)

Cullompton, May 14th, 1847.

At a Meeting held at the White Hart Inn, on Thursday, for the purpose of taking into consideration the distress of the Poor of this Parish, and the best means of providing for them—

It was resolved, "That it is the opinion of this Meeting that the actual wants of the Poor, more particularly in Bread Food are great, and require our sympathy and attention, to alleviate to the extent of our means; but at the same time, this Meeting deprecates the illegal and violent conduct of certain persons, in attacking the Houses of Mr. TROOD, Mr. JUSTICE, and Mr. SELLWOOD. If any repetition of violence occur, the energies of the Subscribers will be checked, the intended relief will be discontinued, and the persons requiring it, will be left to the ordinary course of the Poor Laws."

FROST, PRINTER, (CIRCULATING LIBRARY,) CULLOMPTON.

90 Cullompton 1847

NOTICE
TO
IMMIGRANTS!!

As there are in our City a number of men with remarkable principles, who go among those who have newly arrived and offer to sell or lease to them the *Public Land* in and about this place, thus imposing upon the unsuspecting. The latter are hereby notified that the vacant land in Sacramento City and vicinity, is open for *ALL*, free of charge ; but, they can make either of the following gentlemen a present of a few thousand dollars, if they have it to spare. Such favors are eagerly sought and exultingly received by them. In fact, some of them are so solicitous in this matter, that, if they are not given *something*, they will *almost not like it*, and even threaten to *sue* people who will not contribute to their support. Those who have made themselves the most notorious, are

Barton Lee,	Prettyman, Barroll & Co.,	Warbass & Co.,
Burnett & Rogers,	A. M. Winn,	J. Sherwood,
Hardin Bigelow,	S. Brannan,	James Queen,
Pearson & Baker,	Hensley, Merrill & King,	Dr. W. G. Deal,
Thomas M'Dowell,	Conn. Mining and Trading Co.,	Eugene F. Gillespie,
R. J. Watson,	Paul, White & Co.,	T. L. Chapman,
J. S. Hambleton,	W. M. Carpenter,	Dewey & Smith,
Starr, Bensley & Co.,	R. Gelston,	E. L. Brown,
	John S. Fowler.	

Sacramento City, June 14, 1850.

"Sacramento Transcript" Print.

By order of the Settlers' Association.

91 Sacramento City 1850

THE
METROPOLITAN
Bread and Flour
COMPANY,
156, Fleet Street,
Established 19th of Febʳ 1825.

This Company beg to inform the Inhabitants of the City of London, that they have fitted up the above extensive Premises, for the purpose of supplying the City (and the respective Subscribers to the above Company,) with Bread and Flour of a PURE, GENUINE AND UNADULTERATED QUALITY, WHICH IS THEIR PRINCIPLE OBJECT.

Also to defeat the Trickery practised on the Corn Exchange,
And thereby more effectually to equalize the PRICE of BREAD,

This of all other Companies will be found to be the most beneficial to the Public, as it will at all times afford a Genuine Article, under those patriotic principles, they Company hope to receive the encouragement of the Public, the Bread will be sold at the Manufactory at the lowest possible Prices, and Subscribers of one Guinea per Year, will have Bread delivered to any part of the City, but such Subscribers will have no joint interest in the Company, such Subscriptions being only to defray the expence of delivery.

This Establishment is conducted under the Management of that well known Patriotic Baker, J. WHITE, and will Open on Saturday, the 19th of February, 1825,

For the Sale of Genuine Bread, AT

8d. per 4lb. Loaf.

EGBARTS, Printer, 16, Shoe Lane, Fleet Street.

92 London 1825

PROCLAMATION.

The inhabitants will in future be required to have a candle or lamp at their front windows at night ready to light in case of alarm, and are desired to secure their doors and lower windows. The Police to see to this.

C. E. GOLD,
Colonel Commanding the Forces
New Zealand.

New Plymouth, 20th April, 1860.

93 New Plymouth, New Zealand 1860

PROCLAMATION.

As it is indispensably necessary that families should leave this Town, they must prepare to embark for such places as shall be decided upon.

By Order,

R. CAREY,
Lieut.-Colonel,
Deputy Adjutant-General.

August 6, 1860.

94 New Plymouth, New Zealand 1860

POLICE NOTICE.
STREET CROSSING SIGNALS.
BRIDGE STREET, NEW PALACE YARD.

CAUTION.   **STOP.**

The Semaphore Arms lowered, and by Night with a Green Light.

The Semaphore Arms extended, and by Night with a Red Light.

By the Signal "CAUTION," all persons in charge of Vehicles and Horses are warned to pass over the Crossing with care, and due regard to the safety of Foot Passengers.

The Signal "STOP," will only be displayed when it is necessary that Vehicles and Horses shall be actually stopped on each side of the Crossing, to allow the passage of Persons on Foot; notice being thus given to all persons in charge of Vehicles and Horses to stop clear of the Crossing.

RICHARD MAYNE,

Commissioner of Police of the Metropolis.

95 London 1868

GAS MONOPOLY.
TO THE
CHRIST CHURCH, RECTORY,
AND
ST. MARY'S DISTRICTS,
OF
ST. MARYLEBONE,
RATE-PAYERS AND GAS CONSUMERS.

FELLOW RATE-PAYERS AND GAS CONSUMERS

Under the specious pretence of encouraging competition in the supply of Gas to this important Parish a clique in the district of ALL SOULS has secured to their neighbourhood, and part of these districts which abut on Oxford Street the exclusive benefit arising from Competition, and thereby leaving the entire of Christ Church, and nearly the whole of the Rectory and St. Mary's to the tender mercies of the Imperial Monopolists.

On Saturday last the same parties in the Vestry passed a Resolution to allow the Western Company a similar privilege, viz :—

A SLICE OF THE BEST PAYING PARTS OF THE PARISH.

Fellow Ratepayers we cannot submit to this Let us have fair and honourable Competition over the entire area of the parish.

And this can only be effected by supporting a new Company pledged to do so, and who will charge an uniform price, and NOT MAKE THE POOR MAN PAY MORE *because his Gas for the Winter quarter does not amount to Three Pounds.*

Brother Ratepayers! attend the Meeting TO-MORROW in the School Rooms, at the Workhouse, at 2 o'clock, and DEFEND YOUR OWN INTERESTS.

In haste, I am Brother Rate-Payers,

Yours respectfully,

W. M. CAPEL,

31, Lower William Street, Portland Town,
October, 28th, 1851.

BECKETT, Printer, 45, Marylebone Lane.

97 London 1851

TO THE
BURGESSES
OF THE BOROUGH OF
BLANDFORD FORUM

GENTLEMEN,

The proper determination of the Corporation to prevent the infringement of *public decency and good order* by *improper* Shows and Exhibitions in the Market-Place, has given rise to an organized movement to prevent the re-election of those Councillors who prominently advocated the needed reform.

An active canvass is being made in favor of those persons nominated to fill the places of those going out of office, and it will be for you as Burgesses of the Borough to say whether the Gentlemen who have had the moral courage to advocate *public decency and good order,* and who are eligible for re-election, shall be replaced by those nominated in opposition to them.

Say, gentlemen, which shall it be, Public Decency and Good Order, or Public indifference to either ?

A BURGESS.

Blandford, Oct. 31st, 1862.

W. SHIPP, PRINTER, BLANDFORD.

96 Blandford 1862

TO
Prevent   *Fraud.*
THE REGULAR WAITS,
OF THIS PARISH.

Messrs. J. & W. JACKSON, W. PARK, & J. BEAMOND,

Return their most sincere Thanks for the kindness they have received on former Occasions, and further beg leave to state, to prevent imposition, they have provided themselves with a SILVER Medal, on which are engraved each Person's Name and Instrument, which will correspond with this Bill, as a caution to those who wish to give to the regular Waits, Please to ask to see the Medal.—We shall take the liberty of calling on Boxing Day, and any Gratuity you may please to give will be thankfully received, by your most humble and obedient Servants.

J. Jackson, *French Horn,* 48, Union Street, Middlesex Hospital.

W. Jackson, *Clarionet,* No. 28, Tottenham Street, Fitzroy Square.

W. Parke, *Trombone,*   ditto   ditto

J. Beamond, *Clarionet,* 16, Charles Street, Hampstead Road.

N. B. Music provided by either of the above.

J. Silver, Printer, 59, Upper Mary-le-bone Street, Fitzroy Sq.

98 London *c* 1815

99 London

DOGGETT'S
Coat & Badge.
CAUTION.

WHEREAS on Friday last, the 1st of August instant, on the rowing for the COAT and BADGE, given by the late Mr. THOMAS DOGGETT, for this year, we the undernamed JAMES COLE, and WILLIAM MOUNT, of Saint Catherine's Stairs, Watermen, and JAMES REID, of Blackfriars, Waterman, with others in a Cutter, did wilfully and riotously obstruct two of the Wagermen rowing for the said Prize, by intentionally running athwart them near Old Swan Stairs, and stopping their Boats with a Boat Hook, whereby they were impeded in contending for the Prize, and in such act one of the Wagermen was struck with the Boat Hook, and the whole were obliged to be started a second time, for which outrageous and improper conduct, the FISHMONGERS COMPANY, (who have the sole management of such Wager,) have threatened to prosecute us by Indictment; but in consideration of our severally expressing our contrition for such conduct, promising not to offend in future, making this public apology and paying the expence of advertizing the same, the Company has consented to forego further proceedings against us.

Now we the said JAMES COLE, WILLIAM MOUNT, and JAMES REID, convinced of the illegality of our proceedings, and of the lenity shewn us, do hereby severally apologize to the Fishmongers Company, and ask pardon for our conduct, and promise not to offend again in like manner.

Dated the 4th of August 1823.

                              JAMES COLE,
        The Mark ✕ of WILLIAM MOUNT,
                              J. REID.

NOTICE IS HEREBY GIVEN,

That all person & persons whomsoever, who shall on any future Wager, for DOGGETT'S COAT and BADGE, obstruct any of the rowers for the Prize, or create any riot or disturbance will be prosecuted with the utmost severity of the Law.

                    By order of the Fishmongers Company,
                              JOHN DAVID TOWSE,
Fishmongers Hall,   Clerk.
4th of August 1823.

G. G. & J. H. Abraham, Printers, Clement's Lane, London.

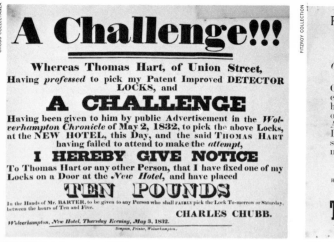

A Challenge!!!

Whereas Thomas Hart, of Union Street,

Having *professed* to pick my Patent Improved DETECTOR LOCKS, and

A CHALLENGE

Having been given to him by public Advertisement in the *Wolverhampton Chronicle* of May 2, 1832, to pick the above Locks, at the NEW HOTEL, this Day, and the said THOMAS HART having failed to attend to make the *attempt*,

I HEREBY GIVE NOTICE

To Thomas Hart or any other Person, that I have fixed one of my Locks on a Door at the *New Hotel*, and have placed

TEN POUNDS

In the Hands of Mr. BARTER, to be given to any Person who shall FAIRLY pick the Lock To-morrow or Saturday, between the hours of Ten and Five.

CHARLES CHUBB.

Wolverhampton, New Hotel, Thursday Evening, May 3, 1832.

Simpson, Printer, Wolverhampton.

100 Wolverhampton 1832

PARLIAMENTARY ELECTION, 1895.

APOLOGY.

COPY.

I, JAMES DUKE, of Great Grimsby, Ironmonger, hereby express my great regret for having uttered certain slanderous statements regarding Mr. Alderman George Doughty, and I hereby beg to withdraw the same, and apologise for having made them.

Dated this 15th day of July, 1895.

Witness:
John Barker, Solicitor,
Great Grimsby.

JAMES DUKE.

TORIES, BEWARE !!

Printed and Published by Richard H. Edwards, Victoria-street, Grimsby.

101 Grimsby 1895

NEWCASTLE UPON TYNE AND CARLISLE

RAILWAY.

THE Directors of the Newcastle upon Tyne and Carlisle Railway Company announce to the Public, with deep Regret, that they are compelled to discontinue, for the present, the Use of Locomotive Engines. At the Time when this great Work, The Newcastle and Carlisle Railway, was originally projected, the Locomotive Engine was of rude Construction, and its practical Utility being doubtful, a Clause was inserted in the Act, prohibiting its Use. The Improvements, which have since taken Place in the Construction of those Engines, have removed all reasonable Objection to them; and have established the Fact, that no Railway can be enjoyed beneficially by the Public without the Use of the Locomotive Steam Engine. Under these Circumstances, the Directors determined to apply to the Legislature for the repeal of the Restrictive Clause, and, in the mean Time, with the Concurrence of the Land Owners, with one Exception, they have used Locomotive Steam Power on that Part of the Line which has been opened. One Individual insists upon the Prohibition being enforced against the Company, and has obtained an Injunction of the Court of Chancery for that Purpose. The Directors therefore have no Alternative but to give up the Use of the Railway, and wait the Result of their Application to the Legislature.

Newcastle upon Tyne, March 28, 1835.

Akenheads, Printers, Newcastle.

102 Newcastle-upon-Tyne 1835

NEWCASTLE
AND
CARLISLE
RAILWAY.

THE DIRECTORS of the **NEWCASTLE UPON TYNE AND CARLISLE RAILWAY** have the liveliest Satisfaction in announcing that Mr Bacon Grey, yielding his legal Rights to the Feeling of the Public, in a Manner highly honourable to himself, has abandoned his Injunction by which the Company is restrained from using Locomotive Engines, and has withdrawn his Opposition to the Bill now before Parliament.

In Consequence of this satisfactory Arrangement the Use of the Railway will be resumed on **WEDNESDAY FIRST**, from which Day the Company's Trains of Carriages will set out at the Hours formerly announced, viz.:—From Blaydon and Hexham each Day at 8 and 11 o'Clock in the Forenoon, and 2 and 5 o'Clock in the Afternoon. For the present the Trains will not travel on Sundays.

MATTHEW PLUMMER,
CHAIRMAN.

Newcastle upon Tyne, 4th May, 1835.

Mitchells, Printers, Newcastle.

TO THE
Inhabitants of St. John's Wood
AND ITS VICINITY.

W. COOMBER,

Of the Marlborough Tavern, St. John's Wood, and the Proprietor of the Marlborough Omnibuses,

Begs leave to return thanks to the Inhabitants and the Public in general, for the liberal support he has hitherto received, and trusts by strict attention and civility on the part of his Servants, to merit a continuance of the same.

He also takes this opportunity of acquainting them, that the City Atlas Proprietors, the Atlas, Paddington, and Bayswater Associations, have entered into a combination, for the express purpose of Running Off the MARLBOROUGH OMNIBUSES by their united efforts, and at a Meeting convened by them in Paddington, on Wednesday, the 5th. day of October, 1853, it was resolved that Nine City Atlas's, running to the Swiss Cottage should be taken off that road, (to the great inconvenience of the Inhabitants of that district) and sent down to the Marlborough, in direct opposition to his Omnibuses

He, W. C. trusts that the Inhabitants and the Public will please bear in mind, that his were the first Omnibuses that started on that line of Road, direct to and from the City and London Bridge Railways, and also that his Fares are **3d.** to and from Tottenham Court Road, and the Great Monopolists, **4d.**

104 London 1853

FOR
London.

NOW LOADING AT EXETER WHARF,
THREE VALUABLE

S.M.A.CKS,

THE

Ministerial, Independent, and Devon's Glory.

Two of which will positively Sail in Fifteen Days, or sooner if Laden.

The Ministerial

Intends taking Placemen, Sinecurists, Pensioners, West India Slaves, Unwieldly Divines, Tithes and Taxes; being heavily laden the last voyage, the Underwriters will not ensure, being certain of her foundering at Sea.

The Independent

Intends Shipping a Valuable Cargo of Old English Oak; the shippers finding it absolutely necessary to repair their Store-houses, the foundation having given way with the last Cargo of the Ministerial.

THE
Devon's Glory,

Is a strong built Vessel, for Passengers only. Several thousand are already on board, being dissatisfied with the enormous charges required by the Ministerial.

Hasten, ye lovers of Freedom, to croud her Decks, the Flag of Freedom is already unfurled, ready to ensure you a glorious Voyage.

Featherstone, Printer, 73, Fore-Street, Exeter.

106 Exeter *c* 1830

Dorchester and Weymouth.
ABOLITION
OF
CHRISTMAS
BOXES.

THE undersigned GROCERS of DORCHESTER and WEYMOUTH beg most respectfully to inform their Customers and the Public, that, for the reasons assigned in the annexed Resolutions, agreed to and adopted by the Grocers of the above named Towns, the practice of giving Christmas Boxes is now abolished. They assure their Friends that at the reduced scale of profits now recognised and adopted, a further continuance of the custom is incompatible with a due regard to the interests of the Public; it is therefore earnestly hoped that the Public generally will approve the joint determination of the Trade of the two Towns, and support them in their resolution to give it effect.

Dated DORCHESTER and WEYMOUTH, 17th Nov., 1852.

The following are the RESOLUTIONS above referred to :—

1st.——That in the opinion of this Meeting the practice of giving away Fruit at Christmas has been gradually changed from its original object and design; and that, as it now exists and is carried out, it is a serious tax on all who are engaged in the trade.

2nd.——That the trade of every district being much more divided than formerly, and profits of trade being in consequence thereof diminished, the existing rate of remuneration does not justify the continuance of the practice.

3rd.——That the present Meeting are unanimously of opinion that the custom should now be abolished; and they hereby pledge themselves that they will neither *directly or indirectly* any longer continue the practice.

DORCHESTER SUBSCRIBERS.

JOHN HAYNE.	THOS. BENNETT.	EDWARD NUTTING
GEORGE HAWKINS.	JOS. MORGAN, Jun.	WILLIAM TRIPP.
WILLIAM EAMES.	J. MASTERS.	JOS. BIRD.
JOHN BISHOP.	L. GROVES.	CHARLES GALPIN.
JOS. MORGAN, Sen.	J. R. JUDD.	J. WINTER.

WEYMOUTH SUBSCRIBERS.

JOHN LUNDIE.	SAMUEL BULL.	JAMES BURBIDGE
GEO. HILL.	SAML. PENNY.	C. BRAIZER.
M. REYNOLDS.	JOHN BROWN.	C. DAMON.
DANIEL PIDGEON.	DAY and STYLE.	JOHN HOPKINS.
JAS. SPOONER and CO.	JOHN C. BEAL.	
J. AYLING.	GEORGE S. VOSS.	

G. SIMONDS, PRINTER, DORSET COUNTY CHRONICLE and SOMERSETSHIRE GAZETTE OFFICE, DORCHESTER.

105 Dorchester 1852

SCARCITY OF CHANGE.

Shopkeepers, Tradesmen, and the Public in general, are respectfully informed, that they may be supplied with

Silver Tokens,

Value ONE SHILLING each,

as an accomodation during the present scarcity of Coin, and that a Bank Note of One Pound will be given in exchange for Twenty of such Tokens, upon application to

HENRY WARD.

Blandford, Sept. 25, 1811.

SIMMONDS, PRINTER, BLANDFORD.

107 Blandford 1811

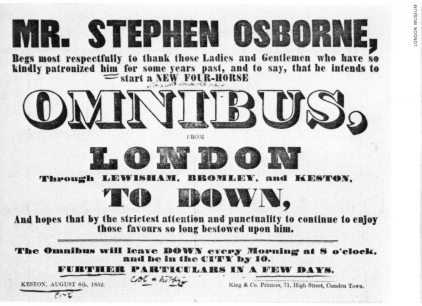

MR. STEPHEN OSBORNE,

Begs most respectfully to thank those Ladies and Gentlemen who have so kindly patronized him for some years past, and to say, that he intends to start a NEW FOUR-HORSE

OMNIBUS,

FROM

LONDON

Through LEWISHAM, BROMLEY, and KESTON,

TO DOWN,

And hopes that by the strictest attention and punctuality to continue to enjoy those favours so long bestowed upon him.

The Omnibus will leave DOWN every Morning at 8 o'clock, and be in the CITY by 10.

FURTHER PARTICULARS IN A FEW DAYS.

KESTON, AUGUST 6th, 1852.   King & Co. Printers, 71, High Street, Camden Town.

108 London 1852

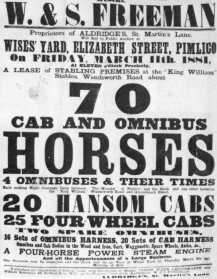

In consequence of the death of Mr. THOMAS ODEY, Cab and Omnibus Proprietor

MESSRS.

W. & S. FREEMAN

Proprietors of ALDRIDGE'S, St. Martin's Lane,
Will Sell by Public Auction at

WISES' YARD, ELIZABETH STREET, PIMLICO

On FRIDAY, MARCH 11th, 1881,

At ELEVEN o'clock Precisely,

A LEASE of STABLING PREMISES at the "King William" Stables, Wandsworth Road, about

70

CAB AND OMNIBUS

HORSES

4 OMNIBUSES & THEIR TIMES

Each making Eight Journeys Daily between "The Monster" at Pimlico and the Bank and one between the "King William," Wandsworth Road and Gracechurch Street.

20 HANSOM CABS

25 FOUR WHEEL CABS

TWO SPARE OMNIBUSES,

16 Sets of OMNIBUS HARNESS, 20 Sets of CAB HARNESS Omnibus and Cab Bodies in the Wood and Iron, Cart, Waggonette, Spare Wheels, Axles, &c.

A FOUR-HORSE POWER STEAM ENGINE

And all the Appurtenances of a Large Business.

The Premises may be inspected and the Stock will be on View at Wises' Yard, on Thursday March 9th, and Morning of Sale.

Particulars and Conditions of Sale of Lease with Catalogues of Messrs. DIXON, WARD LETCHWORTH and WELD Solicitors, 10, Bedford Row, W.C. on the Premises, and of the Auctioneers, W & S Freeman.

109 London 1881

THE FAVORITE.

This Omnibus will start from Down, through Keston and Lewisham, to London, every morning (except Sunday) and returns in the afternoon.

Morning---Leaves Down at 8, Bromley 10 minutes to 9, and arrives in the City at 10 o'Clock.

Afternoon---Leaves Charing-cross at half-past 3; King and Keys, Fleet-st. 20 minutes to 4; Gracechurch-street at 4 punctually; Phœnix Office, King William-street, 10 minutes past 4; Catherine Wheel, Borough, 20 minutes past 4; and Bricklayers' Arms, half-past 4.

Mr. STEPHEN OSBORNE

Would have made no other announcement than the above, had it not been for the uncalled-for attack, and gross falsehood, in a Bill recently issued by Mr. Rabbett. Mr. Osborne always gave the greatest satisfaction until Mr. Rabbett advertised the omnibus for sale. This he was obliged to do. Mr. Osborne offered £160 for it, and both Mr. and Mrs. Rabbett particularly wished at first, (at least they said so,) that Mr. Osborne should have it. Finding that Mr. Osborne really meant it, and fearing that Mr. Hill (the owner of it), would sell it to Mr. O., both Mr. Rabbett and Mr. Worship became sulky and angry with him. Mr. Worship ordered Mr. Osborne off the box one afternoon, and told him to go to the **monkey board**; and one day, when he got to Keston, Mr. Worship took him by the neck, pulled him back, and offered to fight Mr. Osborne. A gentleman, on the omnibus at the time, cried "Shame!" upon Mr. Worship's conduct. But Mr. Osborne declined the offer to fight. Mr. Rabbett, on Friday the 6th inst., used the most profane and filthy language, and said, had he been as young and as strong as Mr. Worship, he would have kicked Mr. O's -----------,* and sent him out of the room. No doubt Mr. R. referred to his weakness occasioned by the gout, and **other things**. Mr. Osborne remained silent under these provocations. He was ashamed of men who could incite a servant to a breach of the peace, and use language of the lowest character.

Mr. Osborne feels that his established character on the road, will ensure to him the kind patronage of the public.

* The language is not fit to print.

110 London *c* 1847

To the SPECIAL CON-STABLES *appointed to preserve the Public Peace during the late Unhappy Disturbances.*

We the undersigned Magistrates acting for the Division of Blandford, return our warmest thanks for the very handsome and spirited manner, in which when called upon, you came forward to protect the Lives and Property of the Public from the Violence and Depredations of evil disposed and misguided Men.

Tranquility being now happily restored. We hereby give you Notice that you are discharged from your duties as SPECIAL CONSTABLES, not doubting that should occasion require it, you will ready again to afford your assistance in defence of Yourselves, your Neighbours, and your Country.

You are required to deliver up your Staves and Tickets, to the Overseers of your respective Parishes, who will send them to Messrs. KING, Clerk to the Magistrates of this Division.

Signed,

J. W. SMITH.
T. H. BASTARD.
J. J. FARQUHARSON.
E. B. PORTMAN.
JOHN JAMES SMITH.
S. BEST.

Blandford, April 12th, 1831.

SHIPP. PRINTER, BLANDFORD.

111 Blandford 1831

TO THE GENTRY, *Clergy, and Freeholders* OF THE COUNTY OF DORSET.

GENTLEMEN,

It gave me great satisfaction to see the Circular issued by the Magistrates of this District, on Saturday last, giving notice of their intention to appoint

Special Constables,

to keep the Peace, at the Election about to take place.

Thus we have an assurance, that the *bludgeon men* will not re-appear; and I entreat all Friends to the great Cause we are supporting, to conduct themselves in the most orderly, quiet, and peaceable manner, when they come to the poll to give their suffrages. Our business is, to hear and be heard—the more our Cause is discussed, the more we promote it.

I have the honour to be,
Brother Freeholders,
Your obliged and faithful Servant,

JOHN CALCRAFT.

Dorchester, 9th May, 1831.

OAKLEY'S PRESS, BLANDFORD.

112 Blandford 1831

DORSET ELECTION
25 Guineas REWARD.

WHEREAS,

A number of Ruffians armed with Bludgeons, committed repeated attacks upon the Freeholders of this County, at the Nomination this day without the slightest provocation.

Notice is hereby Given,

That the above Reward of TWENTY-FIVE GUINEAS is offered to any person or persons who will give such information as may lead to their apprehension, prosecution and conviction.

By Order of

Mr. Calcraft's Committee.

Dated Dorchester, May 7th, 1831.

T. PATCH, PRINTER, DORCHESTER.

113 Dorchester 1831

TWENTY POUNDS REWARD.

Whereas, some Person or Persons, did on SUNDAY MORNING, OCTOBER 12th., between the Hours of Twelve and Four, break into the Shop and Post Office, of W. SHIPP, Bookseller, Blandford, and take therefrom a quantity of Pence, Halfpence, &c., &c.

Whoever will give such information as may lead to the apprehension of the Offender or Offenders, shall on conviction, receive the above REWARD.

W. SHIPP, PRINTER, MARKET-PLACE, BLANDFORD.

114 Blandford 1831

THE BLANDFORD
Reform Committee,

Anxious to preserve as far as may be in their power, the property and peace of this *Town and Neighbourhood* from further violation, and deprecating the scenes of tumult, riot and destruction which have already taken place, earnestly intreat the *Inhabitants of this Town and Neighbourhood* to abstain from those *nightly tumultuous assemblages* which have ed to these breaches of the peace, and to use all their exertions to prevent others from engaging in the same, convinced that such outrages are *disgraceful to Englishmen* and most injurious to the *Cause of Reform.*

Masters and Parents are particularly requested to use their utmost endeavours to keep their children and servants at home.

BLANDFORD, October 19th, 1831.

115 Blandford 1831

116 Blandford 1831

117 Blandford 1831

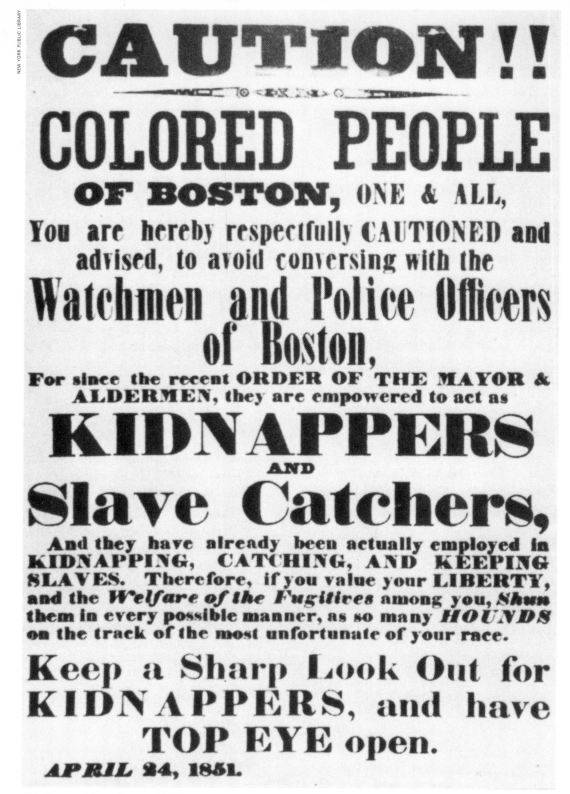

118 Boston, Massachusetts 1851

release him, as he is determined otherwise to proceed to the utmost rigour against any person with whom he is found.'

Thus, in Kingston, Jamaica in 1779, one advertiser. The final sentence leaves the reader unclear as to whether the suspicion is of theft or liberation. Over half a century later, in 1838 [122] the general story remains unchanged.

The runaway slave problem became one of the central issues in the years preceding the American Civil War. Differences between the North and the South over the question of slavery had brought the two regions to division amounting to two separate nations. Many of the slaves escaping from the South had found sanctuary in Northern States, but in 1793, and again in 1850, laws passed by Congress brought about a form of inter-state 'extradition', obliging Northern state police authorities to return runaways to their owners.

The Fugitive Slave Laws served to strengthen and consolidate a massive body of opinion against slavery. The 'underground railroad', a nationwide secret organization set up to aid the runaway, became more active and more efficient. The exact number of escapees is unknown, but between 50,000 and 100,000 slaves are said to have reached freedom through the system.

Theodore Parker, the abolitionist Northern clergyman, was one of the driving forces behind the escape organization. It was he, after the capture and return of a runaway in Boston, who composed and published the famous caution [118] advising Negroes to steer clear of law officers.

It has been said that the arrest and return of runaways, among them the two men referred to in Parker's notice, had as much to do with the precipitation of the Civil War as the controversy over slavery in general.

Last chance to avoid the draft

The war itself, the first major conflict of the industrial era, was epoch-making. It applied mass-production methods to the battlefield. Though still residually cavalry-minded, its generals now disposed full use of the electric telegraph, the railroad, long-range rifle fire, the automatic weapon, the ironclad steamship, the sea mine and the torpedo.

The Civil War years of 1861–65, physically and economically exhausting to both sides, were a gruelling foretaste of 1914–18. Fire-power had become so intense and so sustained that 'digging in'

was the only practical tactic. Entrenchment, prolonged confrontation and economic exhaustion – all characteristics of the war to come – became the obvious strategy.

At first, the matter of getting men to fight presented no problem to either side. Volunteers jammed the recruiting stations. Speed of enrolment was governed not by availability of men but by the capacity of the mobilization machines to cope with them. Recruiting notices appeared everywhere. These too, printed on the new high-speed steam presses, were symptoms of the mass-production era.

In the North, Lincoln appealed to the States of the Union for 75,000 militia. These, he declared, were wanted for action against insurrectionary forces 'too powerful to be suppressed by the ordinary course of judicial proceedings'. Only later, when the Government declared a 'blockade' of Southern ports, was there general recognition that this was not insurrection but civil war; a government might ordinarily close its ports; to 'blockade' them was inescapably an operation of war.

Enlistment on both sides was on a local basis. The phraseology of recruiting notices expressed the literary-cum-military personality of local commanders. Colonel W T Willard, appealing from his New York headquarters, headed his notice *Ho! for the sunny South!* He went on to call on patriots to 'crush Rebellion, and restore the Laws to their protecting influence . . . banishing the demon Rebellion, and ambitious Traitors who have brought this evil day upon us'. Crossed flags of the Union lent an appropriate note of patriotism and gaiety to the Madison-Avenue headline.

In Tennessee, Messrs J B Murray and H C Witt, taking a less euphoric – and flagless – view [123], urged the reader with a snarl: 'Who is so vile, so craven, as not to strike for his native land?' (The use of the word 'Freemen!' as a heading was not merely declamatory: of the Southern States' total population of 9,000,000 some 3,500,000 were slaves.)

In a notice from the headquarters of the Virginian forces [124], with the war only a few weeks old, passions are high: 'Action, action! should be our rallying motto,' says even the small print. 'Let us drive back the invading foot of a brutal and desperate foe, or leave a record to posterity that we died bravely defending our homes and firesides – the honour of our wives and daughters – and the sacred graves of our ancestors!'

The allusion to female honour, with its unspecific but obvious reference to an unprincipled enemy, is a

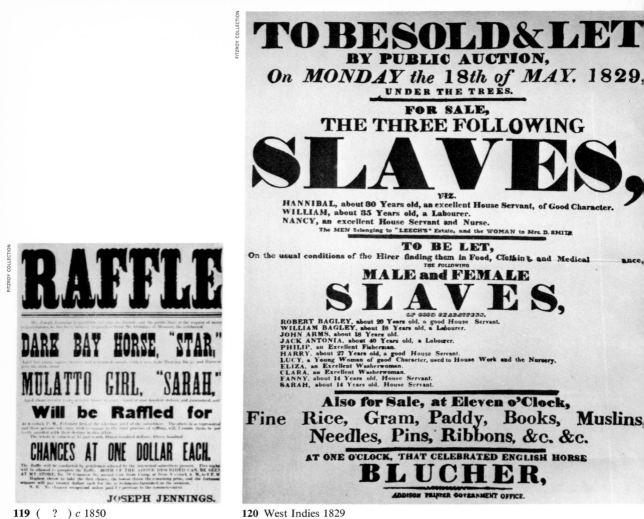

119 (?) c 1850

120 West Indies 1829

121 Virginia 1861

122 Bardstown, Kentucky 1838

universal constant in recruitment literature. Directly or by implication, at one stage or another, it appears in all enlistment campaigns. It emerges again in the Southern States in May of the following year. A 'double' notice reproduces the text of an alleged 'outrageous insult to the women of New Orleans' [126], and calls upon Southern men (with some ambiguity, it must be said) to 'avenge their wrongs'.

In spite of mounting fervour, recruiting notices on both sides shortly began to fail. After the first excitement had abated, enlistment centres emptied. Soon, both in the Confederacy and in the Union, draft laws were introduced to restore intake levels. But these brought active resistance.

In the South there was resentment over the 'substitute' principle, by which it was possible for a conscript to pay someone to join up in his place, and over a provision allowing exemption of one man (one slave-owner) to every twenty Negroes. Both provisions were seen as class privilege.

In the North, there was not only a substitute system (with a highly profitable business of substitute-brokerage as a sideshow), but so-called 'commutation'. By paying $300 a conscript avoided service altogether. As in the South, popular feeling against these provisions was high, and antipathy mounted to actual violence. During the first four months of the law's application in the Union, 98 of the federal registrars employed to apply the law were murdered. In New York, in July 1863, 500 people died in serious fighting that broke out after draft riots. By one means or another, exemption became general. Of the 1,120,000 men who were said to have been officially drafted, only some 40,000 actually joined up.

Enrolment laws, applied only in areas where volunteer appeals had failed, were actually devised not as direct conscription but as an inducement to volunteer. To stave off compulsion, local areas offered bounties to men joining up. (The principle had been applied in the raising of armies throughout history. Not least of its exponents, of recent memory, had been the British.)

The bounty business

Civil War recruitment appeals began to take on the characteristics of reward notices. Coupled with a stirring appeal to patriotism and the suppression of treason and rebellion was an equally stirring mention of a sum of money. Side-slogans stressed the impending axe of conscription: *The Conscript Bill –*
(*page 75*)

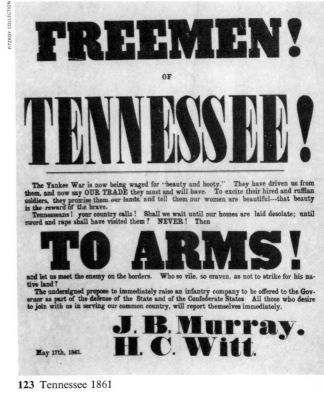

123 Tennessee 1861

124 Staunton, Virginia 1861

MULLIGAN'S BRIGADE!

LAST CHANCE TO AVOID THE DRAFT!

$402 BOUNTY!

TO VETERANS!

$302 to all other VOLUNTEERS!

All Able-bodied Men, between the ages of 18 and 45 Years, who have heretofore served not less than nine months, who shall re-enlist for Regiments in the field, will be deemed Veterans, and will receive one month's pay in advance, and a bounty and premium of $402. To all other recruits, one month's pay in advance, and a bounty and premium of $302 will be paid.

All who wish to join Mulligan's Irish Brigade, now in the field, and to receive the munificent bounties offered by the Government, can have the opportunity by calling at the headquarters of

CAPT. J. J. FITZGERALD

Of the Irish Brigade, 23d Regiment Illinois Volunteers Recruiting Officer, Chicago, Illinois

Each Recruit, Veteran or otherwise, will receive

Seventy-five Dollars Before Leaving General Rendezvous,

and the remainder of the bounty in regular instalments till all is paid. The pay, bounty and premium for three years will average $24 per month, for Veterans; and $21.30 per month for all others.

If the Government shall not require these troops for the full period of Three Years, and they shall be mustered honorably out of the service before the expiration of their term of enlistment, they shall receive UPON BEING MUSTERED OUT the whole amount of BOUNTY remaining unpaid, the same as if the full term had been served.

J. J. FITZGERALD.

Chicago, December, 1863.

Recruiting Officer, cor. North Clark & Kinzie Sts.

BUTLER'S PROCLAMATION

An outrageous insult to the Women of New Orleans.

Southern Men, avenge their wrongs !!!

Head-Quarters, Department of the Gulf,
New Orleans, May 15, 1862.

General Orders, No. 28.

As the Officers and Soldiers of the United States have been subject to repeated insults from the women calling themselves ladies of New Orleans, in return for the most scrupulous non-interference and courtesy on our part, it is ordered that hereafter when any Female shall, by word, gesture, or movement, insult or show contempt for any officer or soldier of the United States, she shall be regarded and held liable to be treated as a woman of the town plying her avocation.

By command of Maj.-Gen. BUTLER,
GEORGE C. STRONG,
A. A. G. Chief of Stables.

REPEAL OF THE UNION !

NATIONAL BALLOT.

No time should be lost in placing MILLIONS of SIGNATURES to the PETITION praying for the restoration of IRELAND'S LEGISLATURE. IT was brought to an end to satisfy ENGLISH JEALOUSY, which witnessed with dismay the strides which a

NATIVE GOVERNMENT

had enabled this Country to make in commerce and manufacturers. It was extinguished, that England might grow rich and Ireland poor; that England might grasp our revenue and use it for her own purposes ; that she might make us, what we really are, Growers of Corn, and Feeders of Cattle, TO PAMPER HER PEOPLE, whilst we ourselves cannot afford to taste the Luxuries.

This must be the condition of every country as well as Ireland whose government is in the hands of others. Let a nation hand over to its rival the making of its Laws, and Poverty, Misery and Degradation must be its lot. FRANCE is governed by Frenchmen, and it is prosperous. Belgium, Holland, Switzerland, Spain, Portugal, are governed by their own sons, & prosperity reigns amongst them

They use the Products of their Fields, and enjoys the Fruits of their industry they have no famines, no exterminations, their people are not flying from misrule and ruin at the rate of 100,000 a-year. England pretends to sympathise with Italy, Hungary, & with Poland, whilst under her own flag a people endure more wrongs than are suffered by all the oppressed nationalities in the world combined. She avows that all her people should have the selection of their own rulers, well *let us test her sincerity on this important question.* No nation in Europe requires a new system of government more than Ireland, and

LET US APPEAL TO ENGLAND'S QUEEN
TO GIVE UP
TO IRISHMEN

The sole right to legislate for this country. England may or may not refuse it. She may act the hypocrite in this as well as in other matters. But at all events let us test her sincerity, and prove to Europe that, after sixty years imperial rule, we are still suffering wrongs and outrages unequalled in the world, and that, having no faith in English promises of justice, no confidence in English legislation, we demand the restoration of our native parliament, that we may rule Ireland, not to pamper Englishmen, but to make

IRISHMEN HAPPY ON THEIR OWN SOIL !!!

☞ The Petition lies for Signatures, at "THE CORK EXAMINER OFFICE," BUTTER EXCHANGE, CHAMBER OF COMMERCE, and at the various Shops throughout the City.

J. BOYLAN PRINTER, CORK.

127 Cork *c* 1861

THE LAND WAR!
NO RENT!

NO LANDLORDS GRASSLAND

Tenant Farmers, now is the time. Now is the hour.
You proved false to the first call made upon you.
REDEEM YOUR CHARACTER NOW.

NO RENT

UNTIL THE SUSPECTS ARE RELEASED.

The man who pays Rent (whether an abatement
is offered or not) while PARNELL, DILLON &c.,
are in Jail, will be looked upon as a Traitor to his
Country and a disgrace to his class.

No RENT, No Compromise, No Landlords' Grassland,
Under any circumstances.

Avoid the Police, and listen not to spying and delu-
ding Bailiffs.

NO RENT! LET THE LANDTHIEVES DO THEIR WORST!

THE LAND FOR THE PEOPLE!

8 Dublin (?) 1881

The Provisional Government
... TO THE ...
CITIZENS OF DUBLIN

The Provisional Government of the Irish Republic salutes
the CITIZENS OF DUBLIN on the momentous occasion of the
proclamation of a

Sovereign Independent Irish State

now in course of being established by Irishmen in Arms.

The Republican forces hold the lines taken up at Twelve
noon on Easter Monday, and nowhere, despite fierce and almost
continuous attacks of the British troops, have the lines been
broken through. The country is rising in answer to Dublin's
call, and the final achievement of Ireland's freedom is now, with
God's help, only a matter of days. The valour, self sacrifice,
and discipline of Irish men and women are about to win for our
country a glorious place among the nations.

Ireland's honour has already been redeemed ; it remains to
vindicate her wisdom and her self-control.

All citizens of Dublin who believe in the right of their
Country to be free will give their allegiance and their loyal help
to the Irish Republic. There is work for everyone: for the men
in the fighting line, and for the women in the provision of food
and first aid. Every Irishman and Irishwoman worthy of the
name will come forward to help their common country in this her
supreme hour.

Able-bodied Citizens can help by building barricades in the
streets to oppose the advance of the British troops. The British
troops have been firing on our women and on our Red Cross.
On the other hand, Irish Regiments in the British Army have
refused to act against their fellow countrymen.

The Provisional Government hopes that its supporters—
which means the vast bulk of the people of Dublin—will preserve
order and self-restraint. Such looting as has already occurred
has been done by hangers-on of the British Army. Ireland must
keep her new honour unsmirched.

We have lived to see an Irish Republic proclaimed. May
we live to establish it firmly, and may our children and our
children's children enjoy the happiness and prosperity which
freedom will bring.

Signed on behalf of the Provisional Government,
P. H. PEARSE,
Commanding in Chief the Forces of the Irish Republic,
and President of the Provisional Government.

129 Dublin 1916

VOTE
Against PONSONBY,
THE
IRISHMAN,
WHO KEEPS
A Popish PRIEST
IN HIS
HOUSE.

SHIPP, PRINTER, BLANDFORD.

30 Blandford 1831

ANTI-CONSCRIPTION
PLEDGE.

The following is a copy of the Pledge:—

"Denying the right of the
British Government to enforce
Compulsory Service in this
Country *we pledge ourselves
solemnly to one another to
resist Conscription* by the
most effective means at our
disposal."

131 Dublin 1916

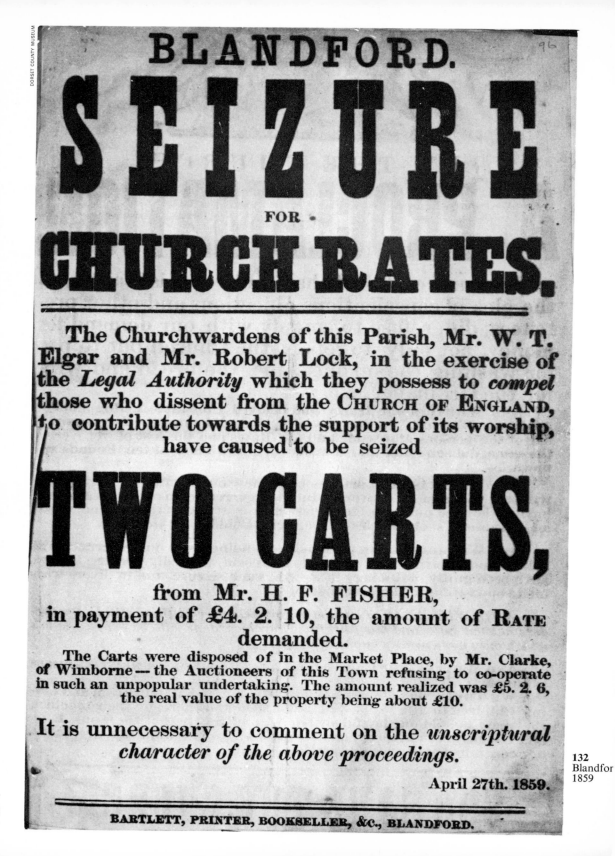

BLANDFORD.
SEIZURE
FOR ·
CHURCH RATES.

The Churchwardens of this Parish, Mr. W. T. Elgar and Mr. Robert Lock, in the exercise of the *Legal Authority* which they possess to *compel* those who dissent from the CHURCH OF ENGLAND, to contribute towards the support of its worship, have caused to be seized

TWO CARTS,

from Mr. H. F. FISHER, in payment of £4. 2. 10, the amount of RATE demanded.

The Carts were disposed of in the Market Place, by Mr. Clarke, of Wimborne — the Auctioneers of this Town refusing to co-operate in such an unpopular undertaking. The amount realized was £5. 2. 6, the real value of the property being about £10.

It is unnecessary to comment on the *unscriptural character of the above proceedings.*

April 27th. 1859.

BARTLETT, PRINTER, BOOKSELLER, &c., BLANDFORD.

132
Blandfor
1859

72

BY THE CHURCH.
A PROCLAMATION.

WHEREAS certain Inhabitants of this Parish, on the plea of conscientious objections and other pretences, did refuse to comply with our demand for money, not only to repair the Church but to pay for washing the surplice, and the bread and wine for the Ordinance, &c. ;

AND WHEREAS our trusty and beloved Constable acting under a "*Distress Warrant*," in that case provided, did enter the *Farm-yard* of one of the persons aforesaid, and for Rates and the cost of recovering the same, did seize and take Two Carts of the Value of ten Pounds and upwards.

AND WHEREAS such articles being now our lawful property, we do will that the same be converted into the current coin of this Realm, and have authorised our respected Auctioneer by stroke of the hammer to sell and dispose of such articles to the highest bidder for the same.

AND WHEREAS sundry persons, not holding us in due reverence, and aiding and abetting the rescuants aforesaid, wickedly declare that we have been guilty of Robbery in making such seizure, and in divers ways incite opposition to the Sale thereof.

AND WHEREAS if such evil counsels prevail there will be few bidders at such Sale, and our faithful Churchwardens will be exposed to loss which only our enemies ought to suffer ;

AND WHEREAS our Church must fall without such CHRISTIAN means of support ;

WE THEREFORE *strictly* enjoin and command all our Loyal and Loving Children to attend the Sale, that then and there, by their biddings, they may uphold our lawful authority, and testify that these our Laws and Usages are in accordance with GOD'S HOLY WORD, and needful for our continued existance and welfare.

GOD SAVE THE CHURCH!

133
Blandford
1859

G.  R.

A PROCLAMATION!

By GEORGE V., King of England

To Our Faithful Irish Subjects,

We are at present engaged in war With Our first cousin, the Emperor of Germany. We hate the Germans, because Our father, Our grandfather, Our grandmother, and all our ancestors were Germans, and every sensible man now-a-days hates his ancestors!

YOU, ALSO, OUR BRAVE IRISH, HAD ANCESTORS blood-thirsty rebels, who wanted to own Ireland for themselves, and be separated from Our Glorious Empire; but our predecessors on the Throne of England (who were all Germans by birth o rby descent) got rid of these narrow-minded savage ancestors of yours. They flogged, hanged, and burned them in '98. They starved them in '48, and brought the food across to feed our Free-born Britons (for Ireland was England's larder then as now). They shipped a few millions who survived the Famine out in Coffin-ships across the Atlantic, and most of them were thrown overboard, and their bones lie whitening at the bottom of the ocean. A few weeks ago, in Dublin, We managed, with the aid of Our Own Scottish Borderers, to let all who had any re-collection of ancestors left, know that We were prepared to clear them out root and branch, and to spare neither women nor children in the clearance.

NOW, OUR BRAVE IRISH, We know you don't want to be reminded that these men were your ancestors, anymore than Our Royal Self do that We are German by blood. WE WANT MEN TO FIGHT THESE GERMANS, and We know from history that the Irish are a Fighting Race. A large number of your Countrymen have been sent to the Front to fight the Germans. THE MOST OF THEM HAVE BEEN KILLED, BUT THEY DIED NOBLY FIGHTING FOR US AND OUR EMPIRE. We want more to fill their places, and ONLY IRISHMEN WILL GET THE POST OF HONOR. Come and volunteer for the Army at once and We will arrange that you will be sent to the Front and Killed; if you are not killed, when you are no longer of any use for fighting, Remember the British Laws—the Poor Laws—have provided for your up-keep in the Workhouses of Ireland.

Remember the Empire comes first and the Poorhouse after, if you survive the War.   GEORGE R.I.

GOD SAVE THE KING

GALE & POLDEN. ALDERSHOT.   D906   5,000,000   8 | 14

How to Avoid It and *Last Chance to Avoid the Draft!* [125]. The 'last-chance' gambit was to see service again in 1915, when Britain's voluntary recruitment had failed to keep pace with demand, and the coming introduction of a call-up was announced.

The bounty idea was an inducement as frankly greed-based as that of William Shirley's scalp tariff and the ordinary reward notice. Its defect was that it roused not only the martial but the commercial instincts of the prospective recruit. Many of them went into business, enlisting, accepting the bounty, deserting and enlisting again elsewhere as often as they could manage to get from place to place. This was the reason for the introduction of the instalment system [125] in which the payment of the bounty was spread over the whole period of the service.

It must be recorded that the British had, from time to time, tried the effect of a straightforward appeal to honour and glory. A recruiting notice put out by His Majesty's Ship *Roebuck* in Philadelphia in 1778, is addressed to 'gentlemen volunteers'. It offers them merely 'the warmest encouragement from the officer appointed to command her'. Another, from the ship *Valiant*, assures recruits that they will be given 'every indulgence that their Merit can entitle them to'.

From Sleaford, in Lincolnshire, also apparently devoid of gift offers, a notice appeals for a 'few generous Britons of pure blood and mettle . . .' It announces that the Second Battalion of the Northumberland Grenadier Regiment 'are now beating up for a Reinforcement of Brave and Loyal Englishmen, to place it in such a situation as to be enabled speedily to share in the glorious service in which the 1st Battalion of the 5th. is at this period engaged, under that distinguished officer, the conqueror of the East, Sir Arthur Wellesley'. The announcement finishes with a bold *God Save the King*. But between this and the body of the text, a discreet bounty mention does appear: 'Fifteen guineas for unlimited service and eleven guineas for limited or seven years service. . . . Three guineas premium to all bringers of recruits . . .'

In 1776, confronted with the 'usurpations of a tyrannical congress', Sir William Howe addresses himself to 'all intrepid able-bodied heroes . . . willing to serve His Majesty King George the Third in Defence of their Country, Laws and Constitution . . .' He offers them not only five dollars, 'besides Arms, Cloathing and Accoutrements, and every other requisite proper to accommodate a gentleman soldier', but a bonus: 'Such spirited Fellows, who are willing to engage, will be rewarded at the end of the War, besides their Laurels, with 50 acres of land, where every gallant hero may retire, and enjoy his Bottle and Lass'. The offer of land, 'for two years' service or during the present Rebellion in America', was exceptional. History has no record of how, if at all, the promise was fulfilled.

Almost simultaneously with the appearance of Sir William's offer, General Washington was also having bounty notices posted. The approaching attendance of a Recruiting Party was announced 'for the purpose of receiving the enrolment of such youth of spirit as may be willing to enter this honourable service'.

'The encouragement at this time, to enlist, is truly liberal and generous, namely a bounty of twelve dollars, an annual and fully sufficient supply of good and handsome cloathing, a daily allowance of a large and ample ration of provisions, together with sixty dollars a year in gold and silver money on account of pay . . .

'Those who may favour this recruiting party with their attendance . . . will have an opportunity of hearing and seeing in a more particular manner, the great advantages which these brave men will have, who shall embrace this opportunity of spending a few happy years in viewing the different parts of this beautiful continent, in the honorable and truly respectable character of a soldier, after which, he may, if he pleases, return home to his friends, with his pockets full of money and his head covered with laurels.' The copywriter finishes, in the approved style of the proclamation, but with due regard for the new regime, *God Save the United States*.

Notice of dissent

The recruiting notice, as well as arousing interest in enlistment, also had the effect of arousing interest in non-enlistment. There were some who felt strongly enough to publish notices of dissent.

In Britain in the 1860s a minority view [137] detailed twelve reasons for not enlisting in the Rifle Volunteers. In Ireland in World War I a British proclamation called forth a counter-proclamation [131]. The same time and place produced 'A Proclamation by George V, King of England' [134], an announcement whose first appearance of respectability extended to a bogus printer's imprint, together with date and quantity code. In Australia [136] another *trompe-l'oeil* effect appeared. This one was the subject of a successful prosecution.

The mock proclamation has long served as a social weapon. In the 1730s, while George II was storm-bound on the English Channel after a visit to his mistress in Hanover, a notice appeared on the gates of St James's Palace: *Lost or Strayed out of this house a man who has left a wife and six children on the parish. Whoever will give any tidings of him to the church warden of St. James's Parish, so that he may be got again, shall receive four shillings and sixpence. N.B. This reward will not be increased, nobody judging him to deserve a crown.*

The public notice or proclamation is a fruitful field for satire; 'ceremoniality' of style and layout lend themselves readily to deflation: in the 1860s, undergraduates at Cambridge published a heavy-weight notice under the heading *Nuisance*. It offered a reward for information leading to the detention of 'persons prowling about the streets at night disturbing the peace and comfort of undergraduates' and 'styling themselves Proctors'.

'To punish all manner of Vice...'

The public notice reflects trends not only in the fields of law and order, emergency and manpower, but in that of personal behaviour. The archives – and indeed certain notices of the present day – reveal that the area of public control may cover much more than crime. The church notice forbidding entry to those who are improperly dressed [142] is a vestigial remnant of an authority once widespread.

In Europe, until the middle of the fifteenth century, when individual sovereign states began to emerge, Church law was universal. Through its own courts, the Church punished offences against its codes, whether moral, spiritual, or matters of simple larceny and mayhem.

Control of the behaviour of the ordinary citizen by the Church often far exceeded that of any civil power. Over and above the exacting of tithes and the administering of punishment for 'secular' offences, the Church applied controls in the field of allegiance and religious observance. Even in such infractions as the use of bad language and playing games on Sunday, the law and judgement of the Church prevailed.

With the passing of time there grew up two distinct bodies of law, the one secular and local, the other ecclesiastical and central. Ultimately, in what was, for the most part, an amicable division of territories, Church and State apportioned responsibilities. Bigamy was immoral and illegal; adultery, which was also immoral, was nevertheless legal.

In the meantime there were anomalies: in some areas the secular law coincided with Church law; in others it did not. Blasphemy, no longer a crime in most areas, remained punishable by the ordinary courts in others. (The last secular prosecution for blasphemy took place in Finland in the 1960s.)

The partnership between Church and State is graphically expressed in the warning put out 'to publicans and others' in Blandford in 1821 [138]. Published, presumably, by the Proper Authorities mentioned in the text, the notice makes it abundantly clear that Church and State see eye to eye in the matter of tippling during the hours of divine service on a Sunday.

Similarly, in the churchyard notice at Wadebridge [151], in the matter of loitering and indecency there is unanimity. (It may be noted however, that the prohibition appears to apply only to loitering and indecency occurring during church services.)

The matter of religious observance and the inviolability of the Sabbath, still, in Britain in the 1970s, an issue in some areas, was a perennial nineteenth-century preoccupation. Not only the law, but the ordinary citizen, expressed attitudes to Sabbath-breaking. The Newcastle essay on the evils of 'Sunday Pleasure Trips' [140] appeared as a private voluntary contribution in the No-Pleasure-On-Sunday campaign.

In its earlier years, the laws on Sunday railway working had been unambiguous. In some areas the Act of Parliament permitting construction of a line specifically required that, in addition to trains coming to a stop during the hours of church services, they must do so at places where passengers could conveniently alight, breaking their journey to attend a nearby church.

Personal behaviour, religious or otherwise, is a major public-notice concern. Certainly the matter of decency and public order has never lost its popular appeal as a topic for printed public comment. The call to the Blandford city fathers of 1862 [96] reflects it as an issue in local politics, with anti-indecency councillors apparently running the risk of defeat at the polls. (References to the 'improper shows and exhibitions in the Market Place', though appearing at length in the newspapers of the time, unfortunately give no clues as to their nature.)

Of all the notices and proclamations of the Victorian era, perhaps none so effectively sets the seal of decency on the monarch's reign as the one published on 21 June 1837 [143].

Europe delivered
The TYRANT'S ARMY Annihilated.

GAZETTE EXTRAORDINARY.

90,000 French Killed, Wounded, and Prisoners in several successive Battles, in which the Talents and Bravery of the Allied Armies were eminently conspicuous.

180 *Pieces of Canon taken,*
Dresden surrendered,
Leipsic taken.

The King of SAXONY and his Family made Prisoners; the Saxon, Baverian, and Wertenburgh Armies all taken.

20 French Generals Killed.

BUONAPARTE RUN AWAY.

135 Dublin 1813

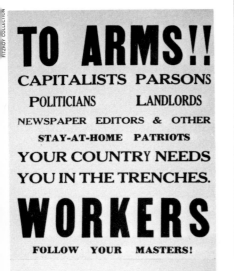

TO ARMS!!
CAPITALISTS PARSONS
POLITICIANS LANDLORDS
NEWSPAPER EDITORS & OTHER
STAY-AT-HOME PATRIOTS
YOUR COUNTRY NEEDS
YOU IN THE TRENCHES.
WORKERS
FOLLOW YOUR MASTERS!

136 Sydney 1915

RIFLE VOLUNTEERS!

TWELVE REASONS
Why thoughtful and serious-minded persons should not join a Rifle Corps.

1.—BECAUSE the Bible says "a soft answer turneth away wrath;" and if this be true, leaden bullets and military slaughterings must produce anger, discord, hatred, revenge, and deadly animosities.

2.—BECAUSE this is a professedly Christian country, and it is utterly inconsistent with true Christian principles to help to perpetuate fightings and feuds between neighbouring countries.

3.—BECAUSE it is lowering to the character of a British Citizen to learn the art of killing for the express purpose of destroying his fellow men.
At a late Meeting at Lewisham, over which the Vicar approvingly presided, it was distinctly stated by one of the speakers that "what they had to do was to get together as many men as they could, and to fit them to kill as many men as possible."

4.—BECAUSE the Army (of which a Rifle Corps is part) is one of the means by which the Aristocracy of the country have enriched themselves at the expense of the inhabitants at large; and it is a fact that nearly every superior Officer in the Rifle Corps which have been formed have been chosen not out of the tax-paying, hard-working, and really brave Citizens, but out of the favored ranks of the upper classes.

5.—BECAUSE if a Rifle Corps is needed, it proves that the Army does not do its duty. There is surely no necessity for our peaceable Citizens to usurp the place of the Army, and become an organized body of voluntary man shooters, when so much money is yearly spent upon the paid and professional destroyers of human life.

6.—BECAUSE it is desirable to foster and encourage peaceable and conciliatory actions and principles, and these it is the object and sworn duty of each Rifleman to renounce and trample under foot.

7.—BECAUSE bad companionship, and the development of evil passions, are inseparably connected with the establishment of a Rifle Corps. How sadly often have drunkenness, revellings, the loss of character, and ruin of body and soul resulted from associations and habits formed on the parade ground.

8.—BECAUSE the paradings, music, and personal glitter, which are necessary to keep up the military ardour, have a highly prejudicial and lowering effect upon the minds of the thoughtless and irreligious, and especially among the youth of our land.

9.—BECAUSE it is a notorious fact that a Rifle Corps attracts the giddy, inconsistent, and wicked, and renders of less avail, if it does not absolutely counteract, the self-denying Christian efforts of Ministers of the Gospel, and Sunday-school teachers.

10.—BECAUSE there is not the slightest chance of any invasion of this country, and it is therefore a pity to put the country to needless expense, and thereby increase taxation; and to excite warlike and wicked passions in our peaceable citizens by the drillings, martial displays, and other proceedings of a Rifle Corps.

11.—BECAUSE it is an undeniable fact that every one must become what is scoffingly called "religious" before he dies, or he will be eternally lost; and because it is an equally undeniable fact that a Rifle Corps is not the medium by which serious impressions are likely to be either awakened or deepened, or a person led to believe in the truths of the Gospel, two of which are—"Thou shalt love thy neighbour as thyself," and "Thou shalt not kill."

12.—BECAUSE all war, whether carried on by guns, cannons, or rifles, is a sad hindrance to all Missionary efforts, and a great stumbling-block in the way of the heathen, whom we desire to Christianize. They cannot understand that that Christianity which they are taught to believe enjoins "Peace on earth and goodwill to man," can sanction wholesale slaughter and butchery of human lives which they see encouraged and perpetrated by Christian England. It is impossible we can perpetuate "peace on earth," or enkindle a feeling of "good will to man," whilst we are giving our time and money to learn the deadly art of war, and to wound and kill the human species with military dispatch and precision.

War is utterly opposed to the whole spirit of the Bible, and it is the duty of every conscientious and Christian patriot and citizen to discourage it in every shape, and to endeavour to hasten the fulfilment of the blessed prophecy, when "the swords shall be turned into ploughshares, and the spears into pruning hooks," and when "nations shall not learn war any more."

N.B. At the present time we have an Army of 200,000 men, and a corresponding number of men in our Navy, and we spend no less a sum than TWENTY-SIX MILLIONS A YEAR for the defence of our hearths, and home, and country. What a useless expenditure of money if the above number of men cannot defend us against a real, and especially against an imaginary foe!

137 Dorchester (?) *c* 1860

This item, running to about a thousand words, and entitled 'A Proclamation for the Encouragement of Piety and Virtue, and for the Preventing and Punishing of Vice, Profaneness and Immorality' delivers a sound rebuke to the nation as a whole.

'We have thought fit,' says the Queen, 'by the advice of our Privy Council, to issue this Our Royal Proclamation, and do hereby declare our Royal Purpose and resolution to discountenance and punish all manner of vice and profaneness, and immorality, in all persons of whatsoever degree or quality within this our Realm . . .'

Her Majesty moves on to matters of detail, turning a searching eye on keepers of taverns, chocolate-houses and coffee-houses and inveighing against blasphemy, and profaneness, playing dice, cards, or any other games whatsoever on a Sunday, serving wine, chocolate, coffee, ale, beer or other liquors, or receiving guests on public house premises during divine service on Sunday.

She has a special word for top people, too: 'We do hereby strictly charge and command all Our Judges, Mayors, Sheriffs, Justices of the Peace and all other Our subjects whom it may concern, to be very vigilant and strict in the discovery and the effectual prosecution and punishment of all persons who shall be guilty of excessive drinking, blasphemy, profane swearing and cursing, and lewdness, profanation of the Lord's Day, or other dissolute, immoral, or disorderly practices . . .'

The phrase 'by the advice of Our Privy Council' must surely be taken literally: the Queen's enumeration of so many sources of profanity, lewdness and dissolution can hardly have derived from her personal knowledge and experience. A second look at the date of the document tends to confirm this view: it appeared on the day after the Queen's accession. She was just over eighteen years of age.

Whether Victoria actually read the text of the proclamation before signing it is a matter for conjecture. Called from her bed in her nightgown by the Archbishop of Canterbury and the Lord Chamberlain, she had been advised of her queenship at five o'clock in the morning of the previous day.

'Her extreme youth and inexperience of the world, concerning her naturally excited great curiosity,' wrote Charles Greville. For the Privy Council meeting on 21 June, at which, presumably, she signed this proclamation, 'there was a considerable assemblage at the Palace, notwithstanding the short notice that was given'. Whether she read the text or not, it left a mark on the country that lingers still.

In its pursuit of good order and behaviour, nineteenth-century Authority is ever mindful of the dangers of too loose a rein; the problem of servants and the working classes is a continuing worry. In the public notice, albeit by reflection, the failings of the lower orders appear in detail. Indiscipline, bad manners, carelessness, lack of hygiene and inherent dishonesty – these and other sins shine forth with dazzling clarity.

Most troublesome of all (and least susceptible of the sanction of wage-withdrawal) are the hawker, the beggar, the old-clothes man and the street-urchin. With these classes, society waged a permanent rearguard war of prohibition.

The servant problem

Only marginally less troublesome were servants, whose failings range from the illicit removal of vegetables or garden produce and material 'or things of any description' [158] to negligently setting fire to their employers' houses [152]. Entering or leaving by the wrong door was a fringe offence [157], but having visitors on the premises [155] had serious consequences.

The word 'servant' continued in use in Britain without embarrassment until the late 1930s. Even into the 1970s the former title of the National Union of Railwaymen – The Amalgamated Society of Railway Servants – continued to appear on decorative roundels at the Union's headquarters building, and the expression occurs consistently in railway bye-laws and small-print rules and regulations. But on the whole – certainly outside the domestic field – the word is an archaism.

In 1870, when the staff regulations for the Metropolitan Railway were formulated [159], 'servant' was a theme-word. In its second paragraph, in which the servant–passenger relationship is clearly indicated, the company expresses the spirit of the age: 'All servants of the company are required to be at all times civil, obliging and attentive to passengers and others . . . They must give their names and numbers immediately when required to do so. Any man proved guilty of incivility will be severely punished by dismissal or otherwise . . .' Even in the matter of the prohibition of smoking, which staff themselves must observe, they are to impose the restriction on passengers by 'respectfully requesting them to desist'. There were no two ways about the status of the railway servant.

Rules and regulations for employees were standard

printed items for the nineteenth-century business enterprise, large or small. With their counterpart for workhouses, ragged schools and other institutions, they form a major section of the public notice archive. Some of them, however, should be treated with reserve: two items in the present collection [153, 154] though printed in the mid-1850s, and often reproduced as authentic documents, are almost certainly satires, produced and posted up by employees themselves.

The *Notice to Employees* exhibit, with its apparently circumstantial references to Mr Rogers and 'the garden below the second gate', has appeared in at least two distinct typographic settings, and claimed as authentic local productions, in both Britain and Australia. It would seem that Mr Rogers, though originally perhaps an actual person, at some stage achieved the status of a legend. Certainly the last two lines in this notice, and the last two paragraphs in the 'Shop Assistants' one, seem to tip their respective texts over the edge of probability.

(The mock notice has been used by employers, too. In Edinburgh in the early 1800s there appeared a notice allegedly put out by 'a newly formed Society of Housemaids', in which strike action is threatened if demands are not conceded. Among the demands, which are listed, is the right to an *annual* hand-over of mistresses' second-best clothes, instead of having to wait for them to become noticeably worn out.)

Authentic or not, the tenor of the 'Notice to Employees' items is clearly a reflection of the times in which they appeared. And it may be noted that as recently as the turn of the previous century the Surveyor of the General Post Office had warned post-boys of the penalty for loitering on the road, mispending time or allowing unauthorized persons to ride: 'Every such offender shall, on Conviction before One Justice, be committed to the House of Correction, and confined to hard labour for one month. The notice carried an added threat in the form of an invitation to tale-bearers: '. . . it is hoped and requested . . . that all Persons who may observe any Post-boy or Rider, offending as aforesaid, will give immediate notice to Johnson Wilkinson, Surveyor of the General Post Office.'

And in the matter of tale-bearing and general surveillance, the Secretary of the Post Office had occasion to put out a notice in July 1816 [164] in which he reminded Postmasters that they were to keep an eye open for 'all remarkable occurrences within their Districts' so that he might in turn inform His Majesty's Principal Secretaries of State. It is evident that the postal service was still viewed, even at this date, as a medieval intelligence network with control responsibilities extending farther than the employee.

No less autocratic than the attitude of the ordinary employer to employee was that of the landlord to rural tenant. Here the twin role of employer and landlord had a double edge. In Ireland, as the terms of Laurence Waldron's announcement of 1854 indicate [83], the landlord's role was close to that of royalty. At Santry Village, too [162], there was little question as to where authority lay, and the 'labourers of Sir Charles Domville' signed agreement to a schedule of fines for offences [160] before they started work.

The notion of local tariffs of fines was well-established in Ireland: 'Trespass Rates' for the county of Roscommon in 1815 [163] prescribed fixed penalties, with a sliding scale based on the kind of animal and the quality of the land involved. As well as its Irish phraseology ('each goat to pay for every offence of trespass . . .') the reader observes the treble penalty reserved for landless tenants ('those who do not occupy any land') whose animals may graze only at the sides of the roads.

The railway notice

The coming of the railways brought the biggest glut of notices that society had ever seen. With its multifariousness, its complexities of mechanical and passenger control and its unheard-of physical dangers, it produced more threats, warnings, injunctions and persuasions than any other single human activity.

Though prolific of print and paper, the railway era also produced the more durable media – the three-dimensional wood-letter notice, the metal casting and the vitreous enamel sign. The railways, it may be said, put the notice business on a firmly permanent footing.

Thrusting and aggressive from the first in the texts of their notices the railways long maintained their offensive/defensive air of crisp command. Staff and customers alike were viewed with distinct suspicion. Even among passengers (notwithstanding staff injunctions to courtesy) there were evil elements. Indiscipline, foolhardiness and downright dishonesty threatened at every hand.

It is a matter of historical fact that in return the public view of the railways was the same, only more

(*page 95*)

March 26th 1821

TO PUBLICANS

And Others.

WHEREAS ROBERT WILSON, of the *White Hart Public House,* in this Town, was on Saturday last, convicted by the Magistrates, of having permitted *Tippling in his House during Divine Service on a Sunday,* and Fined Ten Shillings, whereby he is disabled from holding any Ale Licence during the next Three Years.

THIS IS TO CAUTION

All Owners of Public Houses, as well as Publicans, within this Town and Parish, that the Proper Authorities are determined to use all legal means in their power, to put a stop to a practice so very disgraceful to those who permit it, and so extremely injurious to the morals of the people.

Blandford, March 26th, 1821.

SHIPP, PRINTER, BOOKSELLER, &c. BLANDFORD.

138 Blandford 1831

THE POST-OFFICE

Is always open for the reception of Letters, except at the time of MAKING UP, that is, precisely at **Six to half-past Six o'clock,** IN THE MORNING.

No Letters or Papers delivered till they are all Sorted.

NO ANSWER GIVEN ON A

SUNDAY,

From TEN o'clock till ONE, and from TWO till FIVE in the Evening.

AUG. GODBY, *Surveyor, G. P. O.*

SEPTEMBER 28, 1819.

139 London 1819

SUNDAY PLEASURE TRIPS

"Keep the Sabbath Day to sanctify it, as the Lord thy God hath commanded thee." *Deuteronomy, v. 12.*

Reader,
Such is the law of God, and is it for the creature to defy the authority of the Creator? The Most High God, the God of heaven and earth, the God who gave his Son to die for you, the God who has power to cast both soul and body into hell, has forbidden you to take your pleasure upon that day which he has sanctified and claims as his own.

He commands you to remember the Sabbath day to keep it holy. He commands you to turn away your foot from the Sabbath, from doing your pleasure on his holy day. He commands you to call the Sabbath a delight, the holy of the Lord, honourable. Will you refuse to obey the God that made you, and prefer your pleasure or your gain to his commandment?

"Be not deceived, God will not be mocked, whatsoever a man soweth, that shall he also reap. He that soweth to the flesh shall of the flesh reap corruption, and he that soweth to the spirit shall of the spirit reap life everlasting." *Exod. xx. 8—11. Isaiah, lviii. 13. Jerem. xvii. 21—27.*

NEWCASTLE. PRINTED BY PATTISON AND ROSS, 68, PILGRIM-STREET.

140 Newcastle-upon-Tyne *c* 1870

NOTICE

The Society for the Protection of Youth in Venice

Kindly requests all citizens and visitors to wear garments which are in accordance with the moral sensibility of our young people and with the propriety of our city, which, being proud of its traditional standard of high morality, cannot approve of scanty and unbecoming clothes.

...città che, ...slovinezza ...enezia nel rispetto dovuto alla in...ondibile tradizione ...nell'armonia ed al decoro della la s...atura di ...di signorilità, della sua incon...vesti succinte non ammette ...sconvenienti.

VIS

...mité de Venise...

141 Venice *c* 1960

-IT IS FORBIDDEN TO ENTRANCE THE MONASTERY IN SHORTS OR INDECENT CLOTHING.

142 Meteora, Greece 1960

BY THE QUEEN.
A PROCLAMATION,

For the Encouragement of Piety and Virtue, and for the preventing and punishing of Vice, Profaneness, and Immorality.

VICTORIA R.

WE, most seriously and religiously considering, that it is an indispensable duty on Us to be careful, above all other things, to preserve and advance the honor and service of Almighty God, and to discourage and suppress all vice, profaneness, debauchery, and immorality, which are so highly displeasing to God, so great a reproach to Our Religion and Government, and (by means of the frequent ill examples of the practices thereof) have so fatal a tendency to the corruption of many of Our loving subjects, otherwise religiously and virtuously disposed, and which (if not timely remedied) may justly draw down the Divine vengeance on Us and Our Kingdom; We also humbly acknowledging that We cannot expect the blessing and goodness of Almighty God (by whom Kings reign and on which We entirely rely) to make Our Reign happy and prosperous to Ourself and Our People, without a religious observance of God's holy laws; to the intent therefore, that religion, piety, and good manners may (according to Our most hearty desire) flourish and increase under Our Administration and Government, We have thought fit, by the advice of Our Privy Council, to issue this Our Royal Proclamation, and do hereby declare Our Royal purpose and resolution to discountenance and punish all manner of vice, profaneness, and immorality, in all Persons of whatsoever degree or quality within this Our Realm, and particularly in such as are employed near Our Royal Person; and that for the encouragement of religion and morality, We will, upon all occasions, distinguish Persons of piety and virtue, by marks of Our Royal favor; and We do expect and require, that all Persons of honor or in place of authority will give good example by their own virtue and piety; and to their utmost contribute to the discountenancing Persons of dissolute and debauched lives, that they, being reduced by that means to shame and contempt for their loose and evil actions and behaviour, may be thereby also enforced the sooner to reform their ill habits and practices, and that the visible displeasure of good men towards them may (as far as it is possible) supply what the laws (probably) cannot altogether prevent; and We do hereby strictly enjoin and prohibit all Our loving subjects of what degree or quality soever from playing on the Lord's Day at dice, cards, or any other game whatsoever, either in public or private houses, or other place or places whatsoever; and We do hereby require and command them, and every of them, decently and reverently to attend the worship of God on every Lord's Day, on pain of Our highest displeasure, and of being proceeded against with the utmost rigour that may be by Law: And for the more effectual reforming all such persons who, by reason of their dissolute lives and conversations are a scandal to Our Kingdom; Our further pleasure is, and We do hereby strictly charge and command all Our Judges, Mayors, Sheriffs, Justices of the Peace, and all other Our Officers and Ministers, both Ecclesiastical and Civil, and all other Our subjects whom it may concern, to be very vigilant and strict in the discovery and the effectual prosecution and punishment of all persons who shall be guilty of excessive drinking, blasphemy, profane swearing and cursing, lewdness, profanation of the Lord's Day, or other dissolute, immoral, or disorderly practices; and that they take care also effectually to suppress all public gaming-houses and places, and other lewd and disorderly houses, and to put in execution the Statute made in the twenty-ninth year of the reign of the late King *Charles* the Second, intituled, "An Act for the better observation of the Lord's Day, "commonly called *Sunday ;*" and also so much of an Act of Parliament made in the ninth year of the reign of the late King *William* the Third, intituled "An Act, for the more effectual suppressing of blasphemy "and profaneness," as is now in force, and all other laws now in force for the punishing and suppressing any of the vices aforesaid; and also to suppress and prevent all gaming whatsoever in public or private houses on the Lord's Day; and likewise that they take effectual care to prevent all persons keeping taverns, chocolate-houses, coffee-houses, or other public houses whatsoever, from selling wine, chocolate, coffee, ale, beer, or other liquors, or receiving or permitting guests to be or remain in such their houses, in the time of Divine Service on the Lord's Day, as they will answer it to Almighty God, and upon pain of Our highest displeasure: And, for the more effectual proceeding herein, We do hereby direct and command all Our Judges of Assize and Justices of the Peace to give strict charges at their respective assizes and sessions for the due prosecution and punishment of all persons that shall presume to offend in any of the kinds aforesaid, and also of all persons that, contrary to their duty, shall be remiss or negligent in putting the said laws in execution, and that they do, at their respective assizes and quarter sessions of the peace, cause this Our Royal Proclamation to be publicly read in open Court, immediately before the charge is given; and We do hereby further charge and command every Minister in his respective Parish Church or Chapel, to read or cause to be read this Our Proclamation, at least four times in every year, immediately after Divine Service, and to incite and stir up their respective auditories to the practice of piety and virtue, and the avoiding of all immorality and profaneness: And to the end that all vice and debauchery may be prevented, and religion and virtue practised by all officers, private soldiers, mariners, and others who are employed in Our service by sea and land, We do hereby strictly charge and command all Our Commanders and Officers whatsoever, that they do take care to avoid all profaneness, debauchery, and other immoralities, and that by their own good and virtuous lives and conversations they do set good examples to all such as are under their care and authority, and likewise take care of and inspect the behaviour of all such as are under them, and punish all those who shall be guilty of any of the offences aforesaid, as they will be answerable for the ill consequences of their neglect herein.

Given at Our Court at *St. James's*, this Twenty-first Day of *June*, in the Year of Our Lord One thousand eight hundred and thirty-seven, and in the First Year of Our Reign.

GOD save the QUEEN.

DUBLIN :—PRINTED BY GEORGE AND JOHN GRIERSON,
PRINTERS TO THE QUEEN'S MOST EXCELLENT MAJESTY.

CHRIST CHURCH MEADOW.

The Meadow Keepers and Constables are hereby instructed to prevent the entrance into the Meadow of all beggars, all persons in ragged or very dirty clothes, persons of improper character or who are not decent in appearance and behaviour; and to prevent indecent, rude, or disorderly conduct of every description.

To allow no handcarts, wheelbarrows, no hawkers or persons carrying parcels or bundles so as to obstruct the walks.

To prevent the flying of kites, throwing stones, throwing balls, bowling hoops, shooting arrows, firing guns or pistols, or playing games attended with danger or inconvenience to passers-by; also fishing in the waters, catching birds, bird-nesting or cycling.

To prevent all persons cutting names on, breaking or injuring the seats, shrubs, plants, trees or turf.

To prevent the fastening of boats or rafts to the iron palisading or river wall and to prevent encroachments of every kind by the river-side.

THE GATES WILL CLOSE 7·30. P.M.

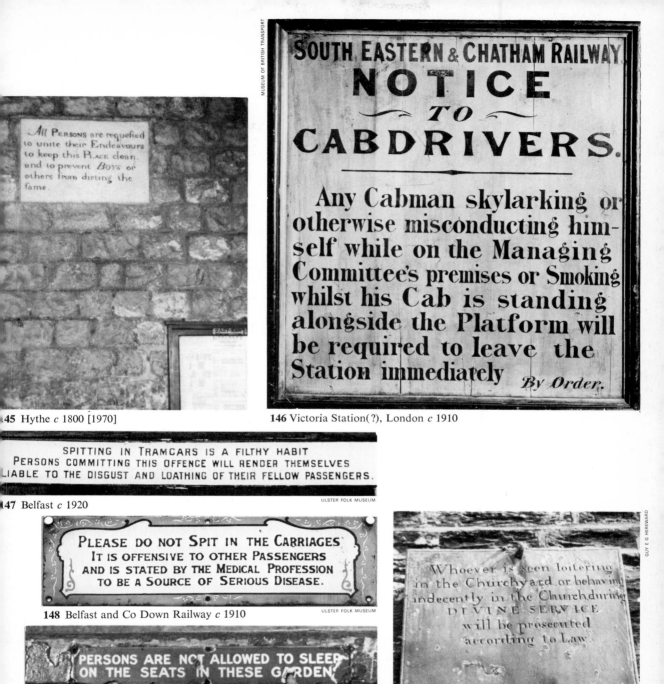

All PERSONS are requested to unite their Endeavours to keep this PLACE clean. and to prevent BOYS or others from dirting the fame.

145 Hythe *c* 1800 [1970]

SOUTH EASTERN & CHATHAM RAILWAY.
NOTICE TO CABDRIVERS.

Any Cabman skylarking or otherwise misconducting himself while on the Managing Committee's premises or Smoking whilst his Cab is standing alongside the Platform will be required to leave the Station immediately *By Order.*

146 Victoria Station(?), London *c* 1910

SPITTING IN TRAMCARS IS A FILTHY HABIT PERSONS COMMITTING THIS OFFENCE WILL RENDER THEMSELVES LIABLE TO THE DISGUST AND LOATHING OF THEIR FELLOW PASSENGERS.

147 Belfast *c* 1920

PLEASE DO NOT SPIT IN THE CARRIAGES IT IS OFFENSIVE TO OTHER PASSENGERS AND IS STATED BY THE MEDICAL PROFESSION TO BE A SOURCE OF SERIOUS DISEASE.

148 Belfast and Co Down Railway *c* 1910

PERSONS ARE NOT ALLOWED TO SLEEP ON THE SEATS IN THESE GARDEN

149 Islington Green, London *c* 1910 [1969]

The PORTER Has Orders To Prevent Old Clothes Men & Others From Calling Articles For Sale Also Rude Children Playing &c. No Horses Allowed Within This Inn

150 Staple Inn, London *c* 1830 [1971]

Whoever is seen loitering in the Churchyard or behaving indecently in the Church during DIVINE SERVICE will be prosecuted according to Law.

151 Egloshayle Church, Wadebridge *c* 1830 [1969]

Abstract

of the Clause in the Act of Parliament of the 6th year of Queen Ann with respect to Servants carelessly setting Fire to Houses.

That

as Fires often happen by the Negligence of Servants Therefore if any menial or other Servant through Negligence or Carelessness shall Fire or cause to be Fired any Dwelling house or Out-house or Houses such Servant or Servants being thereof lawfully convicted by the Oath of one or more credible Witnesses made before two or more Justices of the Peace shall forfeit the Sum of One Hundred Pounds to the Church Wardens of such Parish where such Fire shall happen to be distributed amongst the Sufferers in such Proportions as to the said Church Wardens shall seem just. And in Case of Default or Refusal to pay the same immediately after such Conviction, the same being lawfully demanded by the said Church Wardens That then such Servant or Servants shall by Warrant under the Hand of two or more Justices of the Peace be committed to some Work house or House of Correction as the said Justices shall think fit, for the space of Eighteen Months there to be kept to Hard Labour.

You are desired to put this up in some Publick part of the House.

NOTICE
TO EMPLOYEES

1. Godliness, cleanliness and punctuality are the necessities of a good business.

2. This firm has reduced the hours of work, and the clerical staff will now only have to be present between the hours of 7 a.m. and 6 p.m. on weekdays.

3. Daily prayers will be held each morning in the main office. The clerical staff will be present.

4. Clothing must be of a sober nature. The clerical staff will not disport themselves in raiment of bright colours, nor will they wear hose, unless in good repair.

5. Overshoes and top-coats may not be worn in the office, but neck scarves and headwear may be worn in inclement weather.

6. A stove is provided for the benefit of the clerical staff. Coal and wood must be kept in the locker. It is recommended that each member of the clerical staff bring in 4 pounds of coal each day during cold weather.

7. No member of the clerical staff may leave the room without permission from Mr. Rogers. The calls of nature are permitted and the clerical staff may use the garden below the second gate. This area must be kept in good order.

8. No talking is allowed during business hours.

9. The craving for tobacco, wines or spirits is a human weakness and as such is forbidden to all members of the clerical staff.

10. Now that the hours of business have been so drastically reduced, the partaking of food is only allowed between 11.30 a.m. and noon, but work will not, on any account, cease.

11. Members of the clerical staff will provide their own pens. A new sharpener is available, on application to Mr. Rogers.

12. Mr. Rogers will nominate a senior clerk to be responsible for the cleanliness of the main office and the private office, and all boys and juniors will report to him 40 minutes before prayers, and will remain after closing hours for similar work. Brushes, brooms, scrubbers and soap are provided by the owners.

13. The new increased weekly wages are as hereunder detailed: Junior boys (up to eleven years) 1s. 4d., Boys (to 14 years) 2s. 1d., Juniors 4s. 8d., Junior clerks 8s. 7d., Clerks 10s. 9d., Senior Clerks (after 15 years with owners) 21s.

The owners recognise the generosity of the new Labour Laws, but will expect a great rise in output of work to compensate for these near utopian conditions.

NOTICE

To Shop Assistants

STORE MUST OPEN PROMPTLY
at 6.0 a.m. *until* 9.0 p.m. *all the year round.*

STORE must be swept, counter, base shelves and showcases dusted. Lamps trimmed, filled and chimney cleaned, pens made, doors and windows opened.

A PAIL of water and scuttle of coal must be brought in by each clerk before breakfast, if there is time to do so and attend customers who call.

Any employee who is in the habit of
*SMOKING SPANISH CIGARS,
GETTING SHAVED AT A BARBER'S SHOP,
GOING TO DANCES, AND OTHER SUCH PLACES
OF AMUSEMENT*

*will surely give his employer reason to be suspicious of his INTEGRITY
and alround HONESTY*

Each employee must pay not less than ONE GUINEA per year to the Church, and attend Sunday School every Sunday.

MEN are given one evening a week for courting purposes and two if they go to prayer meetings regularly.

After 14 hours work, spare time should be devoted to reading good literature.

154 (**?**) *c* 1850

155 (**?**) *c* 1900

157 Purbeck House, Swanage 1876 [1969]

General Post-Office,
March 25th, 1793.

SIR,

I HAVE the Honor of the Postmaster General's Commands, to direct you to be very attentive to your Arms, that they are clean, well loaded, and hung handy.

And further, that you do not suffer on any Account whatever, any Person except Superior Officers of this Department of the Post-Office, to ride on your Mail Box, which Mail Box you must never leave unlocked, when the Mail is therein.

If you are ever seen Sleeping while on Duty, you will be dismissed, as you will be for disobeying any Part of these Orders.

THOMAS HASKER.

N.B. The above Orders have been all given before; but I have now the particular Commands of the Postmaster General to repeat them, and to desire you will read over your Instructions.

156 London 1793

158 Purbeck House, Swanage 1876 [1969]

METROPOLITAN RAILWAY.

RULES AND REGULATIONS

TO BE SPECIALLY OBSERVED BY THE

COMPANY'S SERVANTS.

PUBLIC SAFETY. The PUBLIC SAFETY must be the CHIEF CARE of every Servant of the Company. This being mainly dependent upon the proper use and observance of Signals, all Station Inspectors, Signalmen, Guards, Breaksmen, and others, are required to make themselves thoroughly acquainted with all Instructions relating to, and the mode of working all Signals.

SIGNALS.

CIVILITY TO PASSENGERS All Servants of the Company are required to be at all times CIVIL, OBLIGING, and ATTENTIVE to Passengers and others; to make themselves acquainted with the General Instructions, the Times, Description, and Destination of the various Trains, and the General Business of the Line, so as to be prepared to give full and satisfactory replies to all enquiries. They must GIVE THEIR NAMES AND NUMBERS IMMEDIATELY, when required to do so. Any man proved guilty of incivility will be severely punished by dismissal or otherwise.

SMOKING IN CARRIAGES OR STATIONS PROHIBITED SMOKING in the Carriages, or in any part of the Company's premises, is strictly prohibited, and the Servants of the Company are desired to respectfully request Persons who are Smoking to desist.

ATTENDANCE TO DUTY. THE STAFF MUST ATTEND REGULARLY TO DUTY AT THE APPOINTED HOURS in the proper Uniform supplied to them. Great inconvenience is caused by Men coming late or absenting themselves from duty. Men absent through sickness must send a written notice to that effect, together with a Medical Certificate to the Inspector on duty. The Wages of the Men will be stopped during their absence from duty, whether from Sickness or other causes, excepting the "Annual Leave" specially allowed.

MEN ABSENT OR LATE TO DUTY.

ATTENTION TO TRAINS. THE STATION INSPECTORS AND OTHERS attending to the Trains must be ACTIVE and VIGILANT in the performance of their several duties, and CLEAN and NEAT in their persons and Uniforms. PASSENGERS waiting on the Platforms should immediately before the arrival of the Trains be REQUESTED TO TAKE UP CERTAIN POSITIONS on the Platform, so that they may more conveniently and readily take their seats in the different classes of the Trains the moment they arrive; PASSENGERS must also be informed of the DESTINATION of each Train, and the NAME OF THE STATION must always be CLEARLY and LOUDLY called out; and at JUNCTION STATIONS Passengers must be informed for what Trains they will have to change.

CLOSING DOORS GENTLY. THE DOORS OF THE CARRIAGES must be CLOSED QUIETLY and with the GREATEST CARE, so that no part of the person or dress of any Passenger is caught by the door.

READING BOOKS, &c., PROHIBITED All SERVANTS of the Company are PROHIBITED FROM READING Newspapers, Books, &c., while on duty, their sole attention must be given to their proper duties.

SIGNALMEN SPECIALLY CAUTIONED. SIGNALMEN are SPECIALLY CAUTIONED NOT TO READ Newspapers or Books, &c. when on duty, NOR to ALLOW ANY PERSON to be in THE SIGNAL BOX excepting those who are authorised, as their undivided attention must be devoted to the proper working of the Signals under their charge.

RIDING ON CARRIAGE STEPS OR CROSSING THE LINES. All Servants of the Company are cautioned NOT TO RIDE ON THE CARRIAGE STEPS of the Trains, NOR PASS OVER THE BUFFERS BETWEEN THE CARRIAGES, nor PASS ACROSS the LINES in FRONT of an APPROACHING TRAIN.

PERSONS RIDING IN THE BREAK COMPART-MENTS. NO PERSONS except those authorised by SPECIAL PASS are to be ALLOWED TO TRAVEL in the BREAK COMPARTMENTS of the Trains with the Guard or Breaksman, except when there is not sufficient room in the other Carriages, and no Servant of the Company is allowed to travel in any of the Trains unless he is provided with a Ticket or Pass.

LOST PROPERTY ALL ARTICLES OF UNCLAIMED PROPERTY, &c., found in the Trains or on the Premises of the Company, must be given up to the Station Inspector, who will forward the same to the Cloak-Room, Moorgate Street.

DISMISSAL FOR ANY MISCONDUCT Any Servant of the Company will be liable to immediate dismissal for INTOXICATION, or SLEEPING ON DUTY, DISOBEDIENCE OF ORDERS, NEGLIGENCE, or any other MISCONDUCT.

NOTICE TO LEAVE REQUIRED. NO SERVANT is allowed to LEAVE the Company's Service without giving a FORTNIGHT'S NOTICE. In case he shall leave without such Notice, all pay then due to him will be forfeited.

COMPANY'S UNIFORM TO BE RETURNED. When a Man LEAVES THE SERVICE, he must SEND IN THE UNIFORM he has received from the Company to the proper officer, in as clean and perfect condition as possible; if not given up, or if any article has been improperly damaged, the cost will be deducted from any Wages then due to him.

MYLES FENTON,
General Manager.

APRIL, 1870.

FINES

TO BE

IMPOSED ON THE LABOURERS, &c.

OF

Sir CHARLES DOMVILLE, Bart. Santry.

For Riding on a Cart while passing through a Gate, a fine of 1s.

Second offence 5s.

For smoking during work hours, or at any hour, within any Shed, Outhouse, Barn, Stable, Haggard, Privy, Yard, Coach-house, or Room, a fine of 1s.

Second offence 5s.

Third do. subject to dismissal.

For any person neglecting to bring into the shed, (or other place appointed for the purpose) any Implement or Tool which he may have been using during the day, a fine of 1s.

Second offence 5s.

Any person having the custody or charge of any Implement or Tool of any kind, allowing it, or any part or parts thereof to be injured or stolen, will be subject to have same part or parts replaced and made good.

We the undersigned agree to pay any of the above fines we may be subject to.

160 Santry *c* 1820

CAUTION to POST-BOYS.

BY the Act of 5th of *Geo.* III. If any Post-Boy, or Rider, having taken any of His Majesty's Mails, or Bags of Letters, under his Care, to convey to the next Post Town or Stage, shall suffer any other Person (except a Guard) to ride on the Horse or Carriage, or shall Loiter on the Road, and wilfully misspend his Time, so as to retard the Arrival of the said Mails, or Bags of Letters, at the next Post Town or Stage.—Every such Offender shall, on Conviction before One Justice, be committed to the House of Correction, and confined to hard Labour for one Month. All Post-Boys and Riders are therefore desired to take Notice of this, and are hereby cautioned not to fail in the regular Performance of their Duty, otherwise they will most assuredly be punished as the Law directs. And it is hoped and requested, for the Benefit of public Correspondence, that all Persons, who may observe any Post-Boy or Rider, offending as aforesaid, will give immediate Notice to ____ *Johnson Wilkinson*
Surveyor of the General Post-Office.

161 London 1792

SANTRY VILLAGE.

The following Regulations are to be strictly attended to, if not the Occupier of this House being Sir Compton's Labourer, will be turned out:—

No Lodgers are to be taken in.

The House is not to be injured in any way, either by the Tenant or his family, nor are Spirits or Malt Liquor to be sold in it; and as it is to be kept always perfectly clean, the Pig, if there should be one in the Yard, must not, on any pretext whatever, be allowed to go at large, but on the contrary, be always kept shut up.

These Regulations to remain at all times hung up and uninjured in each House, and Sir Compton, or any Person he may authorise, to be at liberty, at all reasonable times, to view and examine the House and Premises.

SANTRY HOUSE.

162 Santry *c* 1820

TRESPASS RATES.

COUNTY OF ROSCOMMON.

At a General Quarter Sessions of the Peace, held at Roscommon, on Thursday, the 12th day of October, 1815,

ORDERED by the Justices of the Peace, then and there assembled, according to the Powers vested in them by Act of Parliament, that the following be the Rates of Trespass to be paid for each and every of the following kinds of Cattle and Beasts, which may be found Trespassing within said County.

	Common Pasture	In Meadow Waste and Fattening Grass	In Corn, Peas, Rape, Vetches, any Green Crop, or Potatoes.
		s. d.	s. d.	s. d.
Each and every Horse, Gelding, Mare, Mule, Ass, Bull, Cow, Bullock, Heifer and Pig to pay for the	1st offence 0 10 2d do. 1 8 3d do. and every other 2 6	1 8 2 6 3 6	2 6 4 2 6 0
Each and every Ram, Sheep, Lamb, and Calf to pay for the	1st offence 0 3 2d do. 0 6 3d do. 0 10	0 6h 1 1 1 8	1 1 2 2 3 9h

	s. d.
Each Goat to pay for every Offence of Trespass in Plantations, as required by the Statutes,	20 0
For any other Trespass,	5 5

If the Party sustaining the Damage by Trespass, shall think that the Damage done exceeds the above Rates, then it may be ascertained by Appraisment, and all Persons who do not occupy any Land, keep Cattle and Graze them on the sides of the Roads, are liable to pay treble the above Rates of Trespass, and all owners of Swine not having an Iron Ring or Staple in the Nose, are liable to pay treble the value of the Damage done by such Swine.

Oliver Cary, Clk.	Edward Crofton, Bt.	Arthur French
Henry Hughes	William Caulfield	James Irwin
Arthur Browne	James W. Lyster	Wm. P. Bowles
George French	Thomas Mahon	Thomas N. Bagot.

Printed by D. DALY, Athlone.

163 Athlone 1815

No. 19.

To all Postmasters.

GENERAL POST OFFICE,
July 4th, 1816.

An Old Instruction was renewed in April, 1812, that all Postmasters should transmit to me, for the Information of His Majesty's Postmaster-General, an immediate Account of all remarkable occurrences within their Districts, that the same may be communicated, if necessary, to His Majesty's Principal Secretaries of State. This has not been invariably attended to, and I am commanded by my Lords to say, that henceforward it will be particularly expected of every Deputy.

I am,

Your assured Friend,

FRANCIS FREELING,
Secretary.

164 London 1816

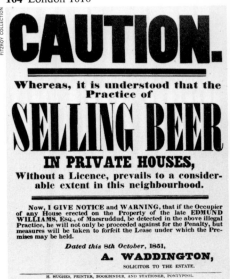

CAUTION.

Whereas, it is understood that the Practice of

SELLING BEER

IN PRIVATE HOUSES,

Without a Licence, prevails to a considerable extent in this neighbourhood.

Now, I GIVE NOTICE and WARNING, that if the Occupier of any House erected on the Property of the late EDMUND WILLIAMS, ESQ., of Maesruddud, be detected in the above illegal Practice, he will not only be proceeded against for the Penalty, but measures will be taken to forfeit the Lease under which the Premises may be held.

Dated this 8th October, 1851,

A. WADDINGTON,

SOLICITOR TO THE ESTATE.

H. HUGHES, PRINTER, BOOKBINDER, AND STATIONER, PONTYPOOL.

165 Pontypool 1851

OGLEFACE Friendly Society's HEARSE.

CONDITIONS on which the OGLEFACE FRIENDLY SOCIETY's HEARSE is Let out.

I. The Body of every Member of the Society, his Wife, or Widow; shall be carried to their place of Interrment, by the Society's Hearse, free of hire.

III. The Parents of Members entered before the 1st of May 1793, and all the Children of every Member still unmarried, shall have their Bodies carried by the Hearse to their place of Interrment for the half of the hire payable by others.

III. When the Hearse is let out to those who are not Members, nor entitled to the above Privileges, there shall be Two Shillings and Sixpence paid, in name of Yoking-money: And Sixpence for every Mile that it travels from the place where it is kept, to the place of Interrment. And if it be not returned the same day that it sets out, the Yoking and Mile Money shall be charged as on the preceding day. The Money to be paid when the Hearse is returned.

IV. If any Necessitous Family shall stand in need of the Hearse, by applying to the Hearse-Keeper by a Line signed by two or three respectable persons, testifying their necessity; that Family so applying, shall have the Hearse at that time for the Yoking-money, to the extent of Six Miles from the Hearse-house. Those who sign the Line, shall be good for damages.

V. If the Hearse shall be damaged when let out, the damage shall be appraised, and those who hired it shall make it good.

VI. Whoever shall hire out the Hearse, (whether they be Members or not) shall pay One Shilling to the Keeper for cleaning it.

A TABLE of the Computed Distance of the different Places of Interrment, in the Neighbourhood, from the Hearse-house of the OGLEFACE FRIENDLY SOCIETY at AVON-BRIDGE-END.

	Miles.	Qrs.
To TORPHICHEN by the Straths,	3	3
To Ditto by Andrew's Yeards and the Wheat Acres,	4	1
To the West end of Ditto Parish, and East to Ditto Churchyard by Craigs,	10	
To MUIRAVONSIDE by Stand-burn and Tirdiff,	4	2
To Ditto by Torphichen,	8	
To Ditto by Boxten,	6	2
To Ditto by Grey-ridge,	5	
To BATHGATE by Torphichen,	6	
To Ditto by Bridge-house,	5	
To Ditto by Borbachly,	5	2
To the Old Church-yard always One Mile more.		
To WHITBURN by Wheat-acres or Hills,	6	
To SHOTTS by Craigs and Blairmucks,	8	2
To LINLITHGOW by Torphichen,	8	
To Ditto by Tirduff,	7	
To Ditto by Bathgate by Torphichen road,	11	1
To Ditto by Bathgate by Cairnnapple road,	10	
To FALKIRK by Glenburn,	6	2
To Ditto by Shieldhill,	7	3
To Ditto by Slamanan Kirk,	10	
To Ditto by Torphichen by Maddiston,	10	3
To SLAMANAN by Pirney Lodge,	3	3
To Ditto by Bulzingdale and Linhouse,	4	
To WEST CALDER by Bathgate and Blackburn,	10	

The SOCIETY have agreed, that the above TABLE shall be the Standard by which their HEARSE shall be Let out in future.—And when the number of miles travelled by the Hearse, cannot be counted by the above Table; that part of the journey that lies beyond the places specified above, shall be left to the computation of the employers.

By Order of the OGLEFACE FRIENDLY SOCIETY,

EASTER-STRATH,
11th May, 1795.

(Signed,)

WILLIAM BRYCE, Præs.
ANDW. SHAW,

166
Easter-Strath
1795

MILTON ABBAS.

TABLE OF PAROCHIAL FEES & CHARGES.

		£	s.	d.
BAPTISMS	Fees are forbidden by law.			
CHURCHING	No fee, but a voluntary Thankoffering.			
PUBLICATION OF BANNS	Vicar		2	6
	Clerk		2	6
MARRIAGE BY BANNS	Vicar		5	0
	Clerk		1	0
MARRIAGE BY LICENSE	Vicar	2	2	0
	Clerk		10	6
BURIAL OF PARISHIONER in ordinary grave	No Fee.			
BURIAL OF NON-PARISHIONER ,,	Vicar	1	1	0
	Clerk		5	0
SEXTON'S CHARGE for digging grave (6ft. in depth) and tolling bell			5	0
NEW VAULT in Churchyard		10	10	0
BRICK GRAVE		1	1	0
FIRST AND EVERY SUBSEQUENT INTERMENT	Vicar	1	1	0
	Clerk		10	6

TOMBSTONES.

All designs to be submitted to the Vicar for approval before being put up.

	£	s.	d.
TOMBSTONE over single grave	5	5	0
RAILINGS OR BORDERS (under 18in. high)	2	2	0
,, ,, (over 18in. high)	10	10	0
FLAT STONE in Churchyard	2	2	0
MURAL TABLET or MONUMENT in Church (not exceeding 10 superficial feet)	5	5	0
(for every additional superficial foot)		10	6
A BRASS in Church	1	1	0
Clerk in all above cases, exceeding £5 5s.		10	6
,, ,, under £5 5s.		5	0
HEADSTONE (not exceeding 2ft. wide) under 2ft. 6in. high		2	6
under 3ft. high		5	0
under 3ft. 6in. high		7	6
over 3ft. 6in. high	2	2	0
HEADSTONES (exceeding 2ft. wide)		Double Fees.	
Clerk, in all cases for Headstones		2	6
ADDITIONAL INSCRIPTION on Head or Flat Stone		2	6
on Tombstone, Monument, Tablet, or Brass		10	6

NON-PARISHIONERS charged double fees.

The following charges are fixed by Act of Parliament :—

	£	s.	d.
STAMPED CERTIFICATE of Baptism, Marriage or Burial		2	7
SEARCHING REGISTER, for first year		1	0
DITTO for every year after the first		0	6
INSPECTION OF TITHE MAP and taking extracts		2	6

The above Table of Parochial Fees and Charges for the Parish of Milton Abbas was drawn up, submitted to and approved of by the Church Vestry, at a Meeting held the 12th day of April, 1887.

Signed on behalf of the Vestry,

CHARLES J. JOHNSTONE, Vicar and Chairman.
COL. HAMBRO, M.P., } Churchwardens.
J. S. TET..
H. FOOKES.
G. PLAYER.

167
Milton Abbas
1887

91

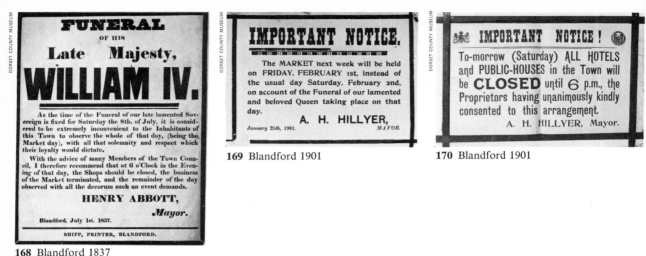

FUNERAL
OF HIS
Late Majesty,
WILLIAM IV.

As the time of the Funeral of our late lamented Sovereign is fixed for Saturday the 8th of July, it is considered to be extremely inconvenient to the Inhabitants of this Town to observe the whole of that day, (being the Market day), with all that solemnity and respect which their loyalty would dictate.

With the advice of many Members of the Town Council, I therefore recommend that at 6 o'Clock in the Evening of that day, the Shops should be closed, the business of the Market terminated, and the remainder of the day observed with all the decorum such an event demands.

HENRY ABBOTT,
Mayor.

Blandford, July 1st. 1837.

SHIPP, PRINTER, BLANDFORD.

168 Blandford 1837

IMPORTANT NOTICE.

The MARKET next week will be held on FRIDAY, FEBRUARY 1st, instead of the usual day Saturday, February 2nd, on account of the Funeral of our lamented and beloved Queen taking place on that day.

January 25th, 1901.

A. H. HILLYER,
MAYOR.

169 Blandford 1901

IMPORTANT NOTICE !

To-morrow (Saturday) ALL HOTELS and PUBLIC-HOUSES in the Town will be **CLOSED** until 6 p.m., the Proprietors having unanimously kindly consented to this arrangement.

A. H. HILLYER, Mayor.

170 Blandford 1901

171 (?) 1865

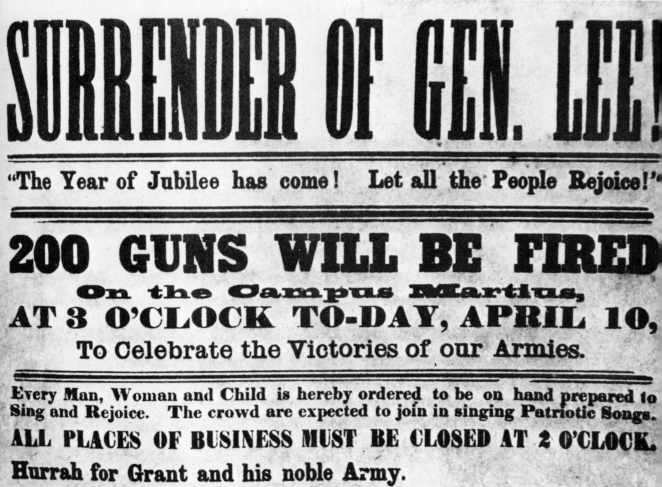

SURRENDER OF GEN. LEE!

"The Year of Jubilee has come!   Let all the People Rejoice!"

200 GUNS WILL BE FIRED
On the Campus Martius,
AT 3 O'CLOCK TO-DAY, APRIL 10,
To Celebrate the Victories of our Armies.

Every Man, Woman and Child is hereby ordered to be on hand prepared to Sing and Rejoice.   The crowd are expected to join in singing Patriotic Songs.

ALL PLACES OF BUSINESS MUST BE CLOSED AT 2 O'CLOCK.

Hurrah for Grant and his noble Army.

By Order of the People.

To the Citzens
OF ILION:

Whereas, on Wednesday, the 19th day of April instant, the funeral obsequies of our late lamented and beloved President, are to be celebrated with becoming ceremonies:

Now, therefore, at the request of numerous citizens, and by order of the Board of Trustees of this village, we earnestly request that all stores and places of

BUSINESS BE CLOSED!

during the whole of said day, and that the citizens refrain from the performance of secular employments.

The public Flags will be displayed at half mast, and at 11½ o'clock A. M., the bells will be tolled until the commencement of

RELIGIOUS SERVICES!

The Citizens are requested to assemble

IN OSGOODS' HALL,

At the hour of 12 M., at which time and place, Religious services will be held, appropriate to the occasion.

It is also respectfully recommended that the citizens have some emblem of mourning displayed from their dwellings and places of business, as expressive of the bereavement which is not only National, but individual, and which has entered, and affects every household and family throughout the entire Republic.

By order of the Trustees,

Dated April 18th, 1865. **CHAS. HARTER, Clerk.**

C 72.41

A FEW WORDS
TO THE PEOPLE OF ENGLAND
ABOUT THE WOODEN BUILDINGS IN THE PARKS;
THE
SQUIBS AND CRACKERS FOR THE PEACE.
AND THE BURNING AWAY OF
Twenty Thousand Pounds, taken from the Taxes without the consent of Parliament.

People of England,
DON'T GO TO THE FIRE-WORKS.

The wooden sheds, and the palings, and the boards against the rails, and the *Fire-works* to be shot off at the end of the present month in the parks, will cost more than *Twenty Thousand Pounds.*

Twenty Thousand Pounds to be wasted, to be blown off into the air, and burnt away in honour of the Peace.

The House of Commons *has not voted* the Twenty Thousand Pounds. **Parliament** *was never asked* about the Buildings.

The Buildings have been put up—the money has been taken from the Taxes without the consent of Parliament.

People of England, You don't want Squibs and Crackers for the Peace.

If the Secretary of War has, of his own accord, put up the Buildings, and the-palings, and the boards upon the rails, let *him* take them down again, and pay for them himself.

If the Secretary of War wants Fire-works, let him have them at his own place, and pay for them out of his own purse.

Insist upon it there shall be no Squibs and Crackers paid for out of the Taxes.

Tell your Members of Parliament not to Vote the Money. Tell them you will **not Vote** for them at the **next election,** if they allow the Secretary at War *to burn away this Twenty Thousand Pounds.*

It would be a disgrace to any grown-up man or woman to be seen at the Fire-works.

Don't go to the Fire-works—let Lord Panmure and the rest of the Government have them, if they must have them, to themselves, and pay for them themselves.

Don't let the money be wasted on Squibs and Crackers. **Let the Twenty Thousand Pounds be given to the maimed and crippled Soldiers of the War.**

There is not *a child* in the kingdom but would cry *shame on the men,* be they who they may, who would forget the *maimed and crippled Soldiers,* and blaze off *Twenty Thousand Pounds* in Squibs and Crackers.

The Queen would give the Twenty Thousand Pounds to the maimed and crippled Soldiers.

The Queen has been amongst them; she has gone to their hospitals; *she* has felt for them, and pitied them, and has *herself* ordered, for a number of them, the best makers to be found, artificial Arms and Legs.

This Twenty Thousand Pounds to be shot up in rockets, and blazed away in red and blue lights, would comfort, for the remainder of his days, many a brave Soldier of the War, *crippled, weakened, maimed, darkened for life.*

This Twenty Thousand Pounds would help to heal the heart-wounds of many a Widow and Orphan of the War.

Be thankful there is Peace—pray it may be a lasting Peace! Remember, in your thoughts of Peace, the men the war has maimed—the homes the war has made desolate. **Have these sheds and palings down.**

Don't let there be a beginning—no one can tell the end of it—*of taking the Taxes for Fire-works,* for sheds, or any other purpose, *without the Consent of Parliament.*

Don't let Twenty Thousand Pounds be burnt away in Squibs and Crackers for the Peace! Protest against the Fire-works. Have these Buildings down!

If Fire-works are to be blazed off; if the *Government must have* their Squibs and Crackers, don't you go to them, don't let your children go. Leave the Parks empty.

Let the Government have their fools'-play of Fire-works all to themselves.

Don't waste your money and time on cabs or cars, and go pushing, and crushing, and keeping out all night, and getting mauled, and done up, and spoiling your clothes to see such a waste of the public Money.

The Government want the people to cheer them. They want the Wrongs of the War, the Hideous Sufferings of the Army, the Loss of Men and Horses, the disgraceful Incompetence of Generals and Officials, and Ministers and Members of Lords and Commons, in the War, to be *blazed out* of the minds of the people by these Squibs and Crackers! **Don't have it.**

Have those Buildings down. Have the Twenty Thousand Pounds for the maimed and wounded, the widows and orphans.

Have no Fire-works for the Peace. You have still to pay the War Taxes.

You have the *doubled Income Tax still.* You have the war taxes on tea, and sugar, and coffee, still.

The War has cost more than a Hundred Millions of Money—*Russia, the breaker of the Peace,* has not been made to pay One Shilling of the Cost of the War.

Let there be no Fire-works for the Peace.—Russia made Turkey pay the cost of the last war; England made China pay for the Chinese war.

Russia should have been made to pay for this War. Let there be no Fire-works! No Twenty Thousand Pounds blown away in Squibs and Crackers.

If the Peace be a great Peace it needs no Fire-works. If it be a little Peace, a weak Peace, a Peace that leaves the Liberties of Europe crippled and unsettled—a Peace that leaves those who were forced into the war to pay for the war—**Twenty Thousand Pounds** blazed away *in Squibs and Crackers* won't *make it a great Peace.*

There is Peace—be thankful. There has been waste enough on the war—waste no money on the Peace.

Don't Illuminate—Don't go to any Fire-works. **Have these Buildings down.** Have those who ordered the sheds and palings made to pay for them.

Have the Twenty Thousand Pounds for the Maimed and Crippled, for the Widows and Orphans of the War. Have no Fire-works. Don't let the Twenty Thousand Pounds be Burnt away.

94

173
London 1856

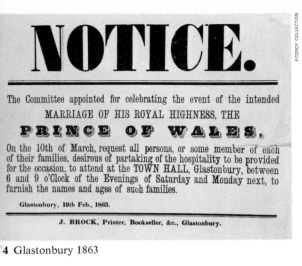

NOTICE.

The Committee appointed for celebrating the event of the intended
MARRIAGE OF HIS ROYAL HIGHNESS, THE
PRINCE OF WALES,
On the 10th of March, request all persons, or some member of each
of their families, desirous of partaking of the hospitality to be provided
for the occasion, to attend at the TOWN HALL, Glastonbury, between
6 and 9 o'Clock of the Evenings of Saturday and Monday next, to
furnish the names and ages of such families.

Glastonbury, 19th Feb., 1863.

J. BROCK, Printer, Bookseller, &c., Glastonbury.

4 Glastonbury 1863

5 Blandford 1820

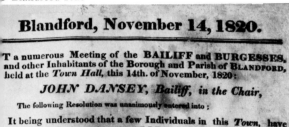

Blandford, November 14, 1820.

A numerous Meeting of the BAILIFF and BURGESSES,
and other Inhabitants of the Borough and Parish of BLANDFORD,
held at the *Town Hall*, this 14th. of November, 1820:

JOHN DANSEY, Bailiff, in the Chair,

The following Resolution was unanimously entered into;

It being understood that a few Individuals in this *Town*, have
expressed their intention to ILLUMINATE their Houses on
WEDNESDAY or some other Evening; it is hereby resolved, that
such a measure will be attended with danger to the peace and good
order of the *Town*; that the BAILIFF shall be supported in any
such measures of precaution as he shall deem necessary, to protect
the Inhabitants; and that if after such precautions violence be offered to the person or property of any peaceable Inhabitant, persons
illuminating their Houses, must look upon themselves as causing
such mischief.

JOHN DANSEY, Bailiff, *Surgeon*	R. BASKETT, *Chemist*
C. J. HOARE, Vicar, *of Blandford*	S. SMITH, *Attorney*
F. R. SPRAGG, *Curate do*	S. CARPENTER, *Builder*
T. WISE, *Dealer of Butter &c.*	G. MOORE, *Attorney*
R. KEYNES, *Dissenting Minister*	M. FISHER, *Draper*
W. FISHER, *Draper*	J. SHIPP, *Bookseller*
T. ROE, *Baker*	E. BARRETT, *Watchmaker*
S. SIMMONDS, *Bookseller*	J. JAMES, *Publican*
H. BIGGS, *Draper*	J. T. KING, *Attorney*
J. BIGGS, *Draper*	J. DURDEN, *Grocer*
R. MUSTON, *Apothecary*	A. S. HODGES, *Hatter*
H. W. JOHNS, *Attorney*	S. PEGLER, *Watchmaker*
W. ROE, *Draper*	W. S. STRADLING, *Ironmonger*
G. SMITH, *Ironmonger*	

N.B. The above Gentlemen with the exception of the five first, are Sworn in SPECIAL CONSTA-
BLES to keep the peace of the Town on this occasion.

TAKE NOTICE,

" By an Act passed last Session of Parliament for the summary Punishment of persons
idly or maliciously committing Trespasses on public or private property it was enacted,

" That any Constable or other Peace Officer and the owners of any property damaged,
spoiled, or spoiled, and his servants or others acting by his authority, or called to his assistance,
without any warrant, may seize, apprehend, and detain any person who has actually committed,
or is in the act of committing any such offence, and take him before a Justice of the Peace."

---

so. For the average man, the image of the companies was compounded of unreliability, cynical disregard for the safety of passengers and a constitutional tendency to swindle its shareholders.

There was much to support the public view. To begin with there had been two periods of 'railway mania'. In these, many thousands of investors lost not only their money but any further confidence in anything over twelve miles an hour. Railway schemes, most of them no more substantial than the South Sea Bubble, had burgeoned by the score. Of those that finally came to anything, many, like George Hudson's 600-mile empire in the North, turned out to be swindles too.

Then there was the matter of accidents. Pushing their profits to the limit, the railway companies economized. Expenditure on such items as signalling equipment, staff wages, track and rolling-stock maintenance, was minimal. Slowly and reluctantly, accident by accident, safety levels were marginally improved. It was close to the turn of the century before even the elementary 'internal communication cord' was introduced.

Staff casualties were enormous. Writing in 1882, Michael Reynolds, himself an engine-driver, recorded some of the facts. Among firemen (whose wages averaged eighteen shillings a week) deaths averaged one a fortnight. There were two serious injuries every week. Board of Trade figures for the year 1889 showed staff deaths at 435 and injuries at 2,769.

Safety, sobriety and decorum

Passenger casualties were little better. Enthusiasm for train rides was muted by knowledge of the figures. Deaths in 1889 were 183; injuries were 1,829; collisions and derailments totalled 163.

A major cause of accidents was excessive hours of duty. The Board of Trade reported that in a period of two years, fourteen collisions were 'more or less due to excessive hours of work on the part of the railway servants'. Recording that duty periods running to 18, 20, 24 and even 27 hours were not uncommon, one expert pointed out that 'there is of course no *practical* difficulty in avoiding long hours . . . but the real difficulty is one of expense. Excessive hours . . . is a source of great saving to the Companies, as thousands of hours are worked every day for which no pay is given.'

Against this background, the *Lies and Mancheater Railway* item [190] appears distinctly relevant. The product of no mean wit (and clearly not unrelated (*page 99*)

Parish of Saint Marylebone.

SUSANNA POLE,

WIDOW OF THE LATE WILLIAM ROLT,

(The Old Established Wait of the above Parish for 55 Years,)

BEGS leave to return her most sincere thanks to those Ladies and Gentlemen whose liberality afforded her a remuneration for the trouble and expense to which she had been put on Christmas last, in providing and conducting the Waits of the above Parish on that occasion; and from whom, as she is about to renew her efforts on the approaching season, she humbly solicits a repetition of the like favours.

S. P. having to contend with opposition, thinks it necessary to state, that no sanction is given by her TO ANY ONE to apply for those favours which her generous Friends may award her; but on such occasion will ATTEND HERSELF, with the Badge of her deceased husband, which has his name, and the words "Mary-le-bone Waits," engraved thereon.

5, Spring Street, Portman Square,
November, 1828.

1st Clarionet, Mr. BUZARD, 100, High Holborn. | 2nd ditto, Mr. BAKER, Clerkenwell Green.
Horn, Mr. GOODERHAM, 18, Kirby Street, Hatton Garden.

PLEASE TO PRESERVE THIS BILL.

FOAT, Printer, 17, John Street, Edgware Road.

176 London 1828

TO THE INHABITANTS OF THE WARDS OF

CORNHILL AND WALBROOK.

CHRISTMAS GIFTS.

LADIES AND GENTLEMEN,

THE Season having again arrived when the *Poor* experience the benevolence of the *Wealthy*;—We, the Collectors of the Dust in the above Wards, respectfully solicit a continuance of your bounty; but to prevent imposition, (as there are many go about who are *not regular Dustmen)* We have authorised our Partner, BILL BISHOP, to receive what Gifts you may please to bestow in behalf of us all. And to prove to you he is the *right* Man, he will produce HIS *License for Slaughtering Horses*, which Business he formerly carried on.

The Dustmen of Cornhill and Walbrook.

GOD SAVE THE KING!!

W. C. MANTZ, Printer, 159, Brick Lane. Spitalfields.

177 London c 1830

TO MY WORTHY

Masters and Mistresses.

LADIES AND GENTLEMEN,

YOUR regular GAS LAMP LIGHTER, belonging to the *City of London Gas Light and Coke Company*, respectfully request you will not bestow your Annual Bounty to any Person but those who can produce a CARD with an impression like the one at the corner of this Bill, as many make a practice of habiting themselves as Lamp Lighters, and calling at your Houses for the sole purpose of obtaining what Gift you may intend to bestow on your regular Lamp Lighter; thereby deceiving you and defrauding him.

Your obedient Servant,

J. Gill **GAS LIGHTER.**

Please do not return this Bill to any one.

1834.

J. FARROW, Printer, 5a, Pudding Lane, near the Monument.

178 London 1834

96

SAINT DUNSTAN IN THE WEST,
26th SEPTEMBER 1800.

There having been Notice given in the Daily Papers,

That the COW-KEEPERS in the Environs of *London* intend to raise

THE PRICE OF MILK

On *Michaelmas Day* next;

THE *Principal* Inhabitants of THIS PARISH, having taken the same into their *Serious Consideration*, on Behalf of the *industrious* POOR, do strongly recommend that EVERY Inhabitant refuse to purchase any MILK for their Families at an *Advanced Price*, there not appearing any *just* Cause for it, as the Produce of GRASS, from the late favorable Rains with which this Country has been so kindly blessed by PROVIDENCE, affords every Prospect to the COW-KEEPER, rather to *lower* than to *advance* such a needful Article to the *Comfort* of the *Poor*, and the Public in General.

Signed by Order of the Meeting,

JOHN WILLIAMS, *Vestry-Clerk.*

N. B. This useful Resolution is recommended to be followed by every Parish in the Metropolis and its Environs.

(T. Jones, Printer, No. 138, Fetter-lane.)

179 London 1800

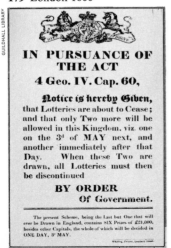

IN PURSUANCE OF
THE ACT
4 Geo. IV. Cap. 60,

𝕹otice is hereby 𝕲iven, that Lotteries are about to Cease; and that only Two more will be allowed in this Kingdom, viz. one on the 3d of MAY next, and another immediately after that Day. When these Two are drawn, all Lotteries must then be discontinued

BY ORDER
Of Government.

The present Scheme, being the Last but One that will ever be Drawn in England, contains SIX Prizes of £21,000, besides other Capitals, the whole of which will be decided in ONE DAY, 3d MAY.

180 London 1823

NOTICE.

All Persons indebted to the late Arthur Heney, are requested to pay the amount of their respective accounts, immediately; otherwise, actions will be commenced against them, for the recovery thereof.

Ulverston, July 17th. 1823.

[*J. Soulby, Printer, Market Place, Ulverston.*]

181 Ulverston 1823

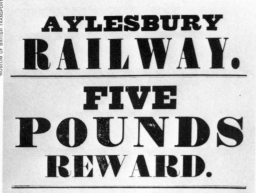

AYLESBURY RAILWAY.

FIVE POUNDS REWARD.

Some evil-disposed Person or Persons have lately *feloniously Stolen and carried away*, a quantity of RAILS, STAKES, and MATERIALS, belonging to the Company, for which any Offender, on Conviction, is liable to Transportation for Seven Years.

Several STAKES driven into the Ground for the purpose of setting out the Line of Railway, have *also been Pulled up and Removed*, by which a Penalty of Five Pounds for each Offence has been incurred, half Payable to the Informer and half to the Company.

The above Reward will be paid on Conviction, in addition to the Penalty, to any Person who will give Evidence sufficient to Convict any Offender guilty of either of the above Crimes, on application to Mr. HATTEN or Mr. ACTON TINDAL, of Aylesbury.

By Order of the Directors.
Aylesbury, *August 18th,* 1838.

May, Printer, Aylesbury.

182 Aylesbury 1838

LANCASTER AND CARLISLE RAILWAY.

To insure the proper service of the Public using the Railway —

The Police have orders not to admit any parties onto the Platform but those going by the Trains. Except persons accompanying, or coming to meet Ladies or Children departing or arriving by the Train, who may be admitted on giving their Names to the Police at the Entrance.

BY ORDER.

AUGUST, 1848.

[J. STEEL, PRINTER, CARLISLE.

183 Carlisle 1848

NEWCASTLE AND CARLISLE Railway.

Notice is hereby Given,

THAT all Persons trespassing on the Railway, or the Works thereof, are liable *to a considerable Penalty* for each Offence. And that the Punishment for doing any Injury or Damage to the said Railway is

Transportation for 7 Years.

THE DIRECTORS GIVE THIS PUBLIC

WARNING,

that they are determined to Prosecute with the utmost Rigour, all Persons who may do any such Injury or Damage to the Railway; and that positive Orders are given to all the Servants of the Company, to give Information against any Persons trespassing thereon.

JOHN ADAMSON,
Clerk to the Company.

Railway Office, Newcastle upon Tyne,
21st August, 1835.

Akenheads, Printers, Newcastle.

185 Newcastle-upon-Tyne 1835

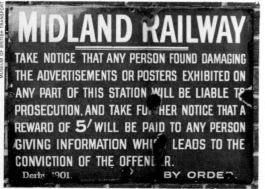

MIDLAND RAILWAY

TAKE NOTICE THAT ANY PERSON FOUND DAMAGING THE ADVERTISEMENTS OR POSTERS EXHIBITED ON ANY PART OF THIS STATION WILL BE LIABLE TO PROSECUTION. AND TAKE FURTHER NOTICE THAT A REWARD OF 5/ WILL BE PAID TO ANY PERSON GIVING INFORMATION WHICH LEADS TO THE CONVICTION OF THE OFFENDER.

Derby 1901.

BY ORDER.

184 Derby 1901

to the coaching trade), this mock notice is among the classics of its kind. From *trompe-l'oeil* title to final dateline (Fleecing Office, Grabbe Hall, Mayhem 1843) it does not miss a trick. It conveys, as no other single document could do, the unsavoury age of the Railway Kings.

From its earliest inception the railway aroused high feelings. Within a few years it was encountering open opposition not only from coaching interests, whose business was faced with extinction, but from conservative opinion at all levels. There was the matter of the desecration of the countryside; the threat to the established order that working-class mobility posed, and the danger of exhausting the country's stocks of metal on unnecessary tracks.

Most of all there was hostility to the working engineers and surveyors who came over the land as an advance guard. Hard-working and hard-drinking, the men of the railway gangs had a reputation for pugnacity. Their head-men and overseers, concerned only to press ahead, had a reputation for ruthlessness.

The combination was a daunting one. Public hostility grew, in some cases, to physical obstruction – sometimes to the point of actual sabotage [182]. Soon the threat was physical violence; it became common for men of the preliminary survey team to be accompanied by bodyguards – recruits from the ranks of the work force that was to follow.

The gangers themselves, many of them veterans of the earlier canal-building campaigns, dug, fought and drank their way through hundreds of miles of terrified rural England. In conditions that no native would have tolerated, they lived and worked in a mobile underworld of their own, rootless, lawless, muscular and alcoholic.

It is not a matter for great surprise that George Stephenson himself, in a notice of the opening of the Stockton and Darlington Railway in 1825, devotes a timorous reference to his workmen. Following a paragraph in which he announces that 'the proprietors and such of the nobility and gentry as may honour them with their Company, will dine precisely at three o'clock at the town-hall, Stockton', there appears the following: 'The Company takes this opportunity of enjoining on all their work-people that Attention to *Sobriety* and *Decorum* which they hitherto had the Pleasure of observing'. There is little doubt that the company had had the pleasure of observing nothing of the sort – and feared the worst.

The unruliness and pugnacity of the railway builders, though feared by their employers, was also often exploited. In America as well as Britain, rivalries between competing companies led to running encounters while work progressed. Occasionally there were pitched battles – even over running rights on finished lines.

The railway builder, by nature a roughneck, and by definition of no fixed abode, was an unpromising prospect for the disciplines of railway working. It was his character, coupled with the commercial ruthlessness of the employers, that largely set the tone of early rules for 'railway servants'. Rule No 1 of the General Regulations of the London and North Western Company (1847) read: 'Each person is to devote himself exclusively to the Company's service, attending during the regulated hours of the day, and residing wherever he may be required.' The spectre of indiscipline was never far away.

Steam at odds with the world

The railways were haunted by other ghosts: the coach, which the train so spectacularly replaced, was an image that refused to go away. The early railway carriage echoed its forerunner in detail – even in its painted name on the coachwork, and 'outside' seats for those accustomed to discomfort. Luggage, as ever, was carried outside too. Equally faithfully, fourth-class carriages echoed the primitive wagons of the rustic poor. The recording of passengers names and destinations was a further inheritance – a direct descendant of the coaching 'way-bill': a book recorded each journey. Metal tokens, and afterwards printed tickets, replaced the book, but the 'booking office' of coaching days remained [195].

The horse was not quite done with; among the railways' better-class customers were those who put their carriages on the Companies' rolling stock, taking their animals in separate trucks, or meeting fresh ones at their destination. The more hardy Gentlemen (or their more hardy Servants) stayed inside their own vehicles throughout the journey.

The horse, with or without proprietor, became a standard item of railway freight. As the Peat Moss Litter notice indicates[201], by the early years of the twentieth century he was a regular customer. At one stage [203] he even achieved the status of a trespasser.

While wooing the public on one hand, on the other the railways hated the sight of them. There were special cheap excursions, there was lighting, curtains and home comfort in carriages; there were footwarmers, 'buffets', and even, finally, lunch-

(*page 105*)

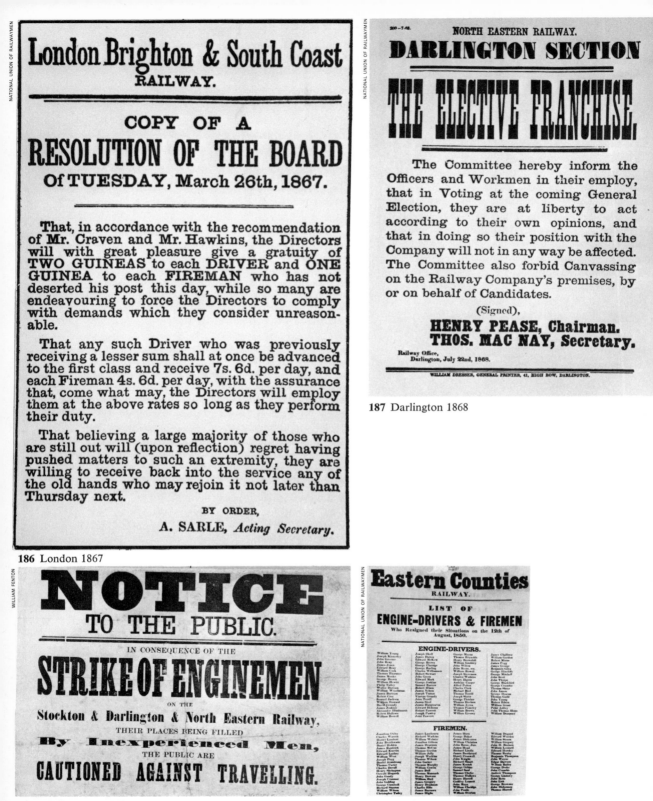

London Brighton & South Coast
RAILWAY.

COPY OF A
RESOLUTION OF THE BOARD
Of TUESDAY, March 26th, 1867.

That, in accordance with the recommendation of Mr. Craven and Mr. Hawkins, the Directors will with great pleasure give a gratuity of **TWO GUINEAS** to each **DRIVER** and **ONE GUINEA** to each **FIREMAN** who has not deserted his post this day, while so many are endeavouring to force the Directors to comply with demands which they consider unreasonable.

That any such Driver who was previously receiving a lesser sum shall at once be advanced to the first class and receive 7s. 6d. per day, and each Fireman 4s. 6d. per day, with the assurance that, come what may, the Directors will employ them at the above rates so long as they perform their duty.

That believing a large majority of those who are still out will (upon reflection) regret having pushed matters to such an extremity, they are willing to receive back into the service any of the old hands who may rejoin it not later than Thursday next.

BY ORDER,
A. SARLE, *Acting Secretary.*

186 London 1867

20—7.48. NORTH EASTERN RAILWAY.
DARLINGTON SECTION
THE ELECTIVE FRANCHISE.

The Committee hereby inform the Officers and Workmen in their employ, that in Voting at the coming General Election, they are at liberty to act according to their own opinions, and that in doing so their position with the Company will not in any way be affected. The Committee also forbid Canvassing on the Railway Company's premises, by or on behalf of Candidates.

(Signed),

HENRY PEASE, Chairman.
THOS. MAC NAY, Secretary.

Railway Office,
Darlington, July 22nd, 1868.

WILLIAM DRESSER, GENERAL PRINTER, 41, HIGH ROW, DARLINGTON.

187 Darlington 1868

NOTICE
TO THE PUBLIC.

IN CONSEQUENCE OF THE

STRIKE OF ENGINEMEN

ON THE

Stockton & Darlington & North Eastern Railway,

THEIR PLACES BEING FILLED

By Inexperienced Men,

THE PUBLIC ARE

CAUTIONED AGAINST TRAVELLING.

188 Darlington *c* 1860

Eastern Counties
RAILWAY.
LIST OF
ENGINE-DRIVERS & FIREMEN
Who Resigned their Situations on the 12th of August, 1850.

ENGINE-DRIVERS.

FIREMEN.

189 London 1850

191 York 1901

192 London 1888

Manchester 1843

193 Derby 1875

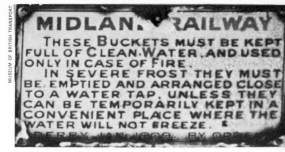

194 Derby 1909

195 (?) c 1900

196 Newcastle-upon-Tyne 1847

NOTICE
BY 8 VIC. CAP. 20. S. 75. ANY PERSON NOT
FASTENING THIS GATE AFTER HAVING
PASSED THROUGH IS LIABLE TO A PENALTY
OF FORTY SHILLINGS.

197 (?) c 1850

LONDON BRIGHTON & SOUTH COAST RAILWAY.

CAUTION TO PASSENGERS

AS TO ALIGHTING FROM TRAINS.—Passengers are cautioned to use great care in alighting from the Carriages; to see that the Train is at the platform, that it is the proper side to alight, and *not to alight till the Train has stopped.*

AS TO LOOKING OUT OF CARRIAGE WINDOWS.—Passengers are also cautioned against putting their heads out of the Carriage Windows when Trains are in motion, and especially *when passing through Tunnels, Bridges, &c.*

THROWING EMPTY BOTTLES OUT OF TRAINS.—Passengers are earnestly requested to abstain from this most objectionable practice, which is attended with much risk and danger to the public, and also to the Company's Staff at Stations, and to the men at work upon the Line.

LIGHTED MATCHES.—Passengers are requested not to carelessly throw away matches in a lighted state, either on the floors of Carriages or out of Carriage Windows, or upon the Platform or Floors of Stations, &c.

COMPARTMENTS FOR SMOKING.—Smoking is only permitted in those compartments of Carriages so designated.

CUSHIONS AND SEATS OF CARRIAGES.—Passengers are requested not to place their feet upon the cushions or seats of the Carriages.

CARRIAGE DOORS & CARRIAGE KEYS.—The locking and unlocking of Carriage Doors should only be done by the Officials of the Company. Passengers are not allowed to use Carriage Keys of their own for this purpose.

London Bridge Terminus.   (By Order)   **J. P. KNIGHT,** *General Manager.*

8 London c 1870

SOUTHERN RAILWAY
THROWING STONES, Etc.
NOTICE IS HEREBY GIVEN

That, under section 98 of the Southern Railway Act 1924 any person who shall unlawfully throw or cause to fall or strike at against into or upon any engine tender carriage or truck used upon or any works or apparatus upon any of the railways now or hereafter belonging or leased to or worked by the Company solely or in conjunction with any other company or companies or to or by any joint committee now or hereafter incorporated or constituted by Act of Parliament on which the Company may be represented any wood stone or other matter or thing likely to cause damage or injury to persons or property shall on conviction be liable to a penalty not exceeding **40/-** and Boys under 14 years of age may, either in addition to or instead of any other punishment, be ordered to be whipped with not more than SIX STROKES OF A BIRCH ROD.

Waterloo Station, London. S.E.1
December, 1924.

By Order.

199 London 1924

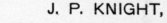

MEN EMPLOYED BY FARMERS MUST NOT CROSS THE MAIN LINES TO FETCH MILK CANS

200 (?) *c* 1900

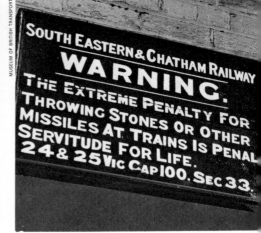

SOUTH EASTERN & CHATHAM RAILWAY
WARNING.
THE EXTREME PENALTY FOR THROWING STONES OR OTHER MISSILES AT TRAINS IS PENAL SERVITUDE FOR LIFE.
24 & 25 VIC CAP 100. SEC 33.

202 (?) *c* 1885

MIDLAND RAILWAY.

INSTRUCTIONS FOR USE OF
PEAT MOSS LITTER.

On receipt the bales must be counted, and the weight tested. Great care must be exercised in handling so as to avoid waste, and the Litter must be stored under cover.

Where there are drain grates in the stable, a wisp of straw must be put in to prevent the Litter getting in and stopping them up. All drains must be examined and flushed at least once a week, and any sediment that may have accumulated must be removed. This is very important.

In putting down bedding, the Litter must be well broken up and spread evenly in the stall, or loose box, to a depth of 5 or 6 inches, which will form a good bed.

Each morning, or more frequently if necessary, all droppings and such portions of the Litter as are saturated with urine, must be carefully removed, and the Litter well turned over, and neatly brushed to the sides of the stalls. Special rakes will be supplied from Stores on application.

When the horse is out of the stable, the Litter must be spread lightly over the full extent of the stall to dry.

Portions of Litter unfit for further use, must be replaced as required by spreading small quantities of fresh Peat, always maintaining a comfortable bed of the depth of 5 or 6 inches.

The weekly consumption of Litter should not exceed 40 lbs. per horse.

Should any new horse at first refuse to lie down, a thin layer of straw may be spread over the Peat, and then it will readily do so after a night or two, when it becomes better acquainted with the nature of the bedding.

A report must be made on the Monthly Horse Stock Summary, which is sent to me, stating what quantity of Peat Moss is on hand, and when fresh supplies are required, 10 days' notice must be given.

HENRY EVANS,
Derby, March, 1912.   CHIEF GOODS MANAGER.

201 Derby 1912

NONE BUT COMPANY'S HORSES ALLOWED TO DRINK AT THIS TROUGH

203 (?) *c* 1900

PLEASE
HURRY ON
FOR THE LIFT

204 (?) *c* 1910

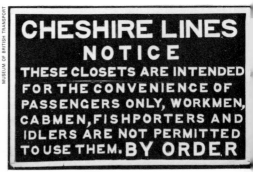

CHESHIRE LINES
NOTICE
THESE CLOSETS ARE INTENDED FOR THE CONVENIENCE OF PASSENGERS ONLY, WORKMEN, CABMEN, FISHPORTERS AND IDLERS ARE NOT PERMITTED TO USE THEM. BY ORDER

205 (?) *c* 1890

baskets [193]. But there were also dire threats: flogging [199], transportation [185] and penal servitude for life [202]. The companies lashed about them with unceasing public-notice fervour.

Every man's hand, it seemed, was against them. Parliament, with its insistence on one cheap train a day in both directions (and on minimum standards of safety and comfort for passengers) was against them. The work force, with its endless capacity for demanding a ten-hour working day, and even going on strike [188], was against them. The individual worker, with his proclivity for reading newspapers in signal boxes and using conveniences designed solely for the use of customers, was against them.

The passenger-public, with its destructive attitude to station advertisements, its habit of throwing bottles out of carriage windows, of decapitating itself by looking out of windows in tunnels, alighting before the train had stopped, and a hundred other misdemeanours, was against them. The lower classes, with their ungrateful response to the provision of special facilities for them [196] were against them. And the criminal classes, who injured and damaged the railway, took parts of it away, and threw stones at it, were against them.

At odds with parliament, public and servants alike, the railways grew up with a permanently suspicious streak. But with maturity, suspicion gave way to a constitutional circumspection. Discipline, however, remained a major concern. In the printed instructions circulated to railmen on the occasion of their majesties' journey from Kings Cross to Edinburgh in 1903, paragraph 16 says: 'Drivers of trains standing in sidings or on adjacent lines waiting for the passing of the Royal Train must, as far as practicable, prevent their engines emitting smoke or blowing off steam, and must not sound the whistle, except in case of emergency, when the Royal Train is passing.' Paragraph 23, which requires that stations on the route be kept clear of all but police and company staff, adds a special note. 'The Servants of the Company are to perform the necessary work on the platforms without noise, and no cheering or other demonstration must be allowed.'

'You are invited to come forward . . .

If discipline and control are crucial to the running of a railway, they are no less so in the running of a war. In the mass manipulation of men and war materials, the public notice moves into perceptibly higher gear.

In later times the communication of control was effected largely through the newspaper. More recently still the medium is radio and television. But in the eighteenth century and nineteenth century the accent was almost entirely on the public notice; the notice was an essential item of war logistics.

Its widespread use in recruitment and mobilization has been referred to: the appeal for volunteers and the formal call-up notice are part of the ordinary mechanism of war. But in a wide range of supplementary war activities the notice also operates. Not least is the requisitioning of weapons, transport and other materials, and the enlistment of civilian help.

Typical is an 'address' published in England at the time of the threatened invasion by Napoleon. Directed to 'all ranks and descriptions of Englishmen', it calls for recruits to the armed force: 'The French are now assembling the largest Force that was ever prepared to invade this Kingdom . . . You are invited to come forward . . . by entering your Names on the Lists sent to each Parish . . .' It calls however not only for military recruits but for civilian workers: 'Pioneers and Labourers' and 'Drivers of Waggons' are needed, the labourers for 'levelling or breaking up Roads' and the drivers for unspecified duties. Labourers are to get eighteen pence a day ('each man to supply his own Pick axes, Spades, Shovels, Bill-hooks or other working Implements'), and drivers are offered 'the same Pay as they receive in the Service of their Masters'.

In a footnote of down-to-earth practicality the notice carries instructions for its own distribution: 'One copy to be affixed to the Church-Door – One Copy to be affixed on the most Public Place in the Parish etc – One Copy is desired to be put up in each Public-house in the Parish – And the other Copies among such inhabitants who are most likely to engage in the Services above-mentioned.' Though primitive, the instruction embodies the whole notion of systematic civilian communication.

Occasionally the impulse to civilian involvement appears to originate not from the centre but from the constituency. In the Ramsgate declaration of loyalty [206] central government is invited to state its requirements. In the instance in question, published on 5 August 1803, a response appeared in a week. It was addressed to the Deputy. It stated that 'in consequence of the difficulty which may attend immediately issuing Arms from His Majesty's Stores to the full extent necessary for training and exercising the very large additional force now raising throughout the Kingdom, His Majesty is desirous of resorting to the Zeal and Public Spirit of all persons possessed of Musquets or guns of any other description, who may be induced for a time voluntarily to Furnish them in Aid of the Public Service'. It was further requested that 'you will call upon all persons within your Vill to make a Return of the Arms (as above described) in their respective possession, stating what Number each person is willing to spare for the Public Service, and for what time . . .' The form carries spaces at the foot headed respectively, *Name, Musquet, Gun,* in which the zeal and public spirit of the citizen may move him to enter his patriotic contribution.

Notices in this vein clearly foreshadow the systematic requisitioning and mobilizing of all civilian resources in total war. With the development of industrialization and mass technologies the role of 'civilian-power' was soon to be viewed with as much interest as purely military power. By the end of the century, when war had become as mechanized as peace, the whole of a nation's economy, and the whole of its civilian strength, was brought into the fight. Civilian controls – prohibitions, instructions and admonitions – multiplied. So did subjects for the public notice.

In the early months of World War I, any residual notion of warfare as the sole prerogative of armies finally faded. The concept of the Home Front, with civilian population actually at risk through air attack, made the case for civilian control complete.

In addition to mandatory food and fuel conservation, there emerged the idea of Civil Defence. The publishing of a 'Police Notice as to Lights in London' [218], inadequate as its provisions appear by blackout standards of World War II, marked a significant step. The public at large were at war.

By 1939 civilians everywhere had accepted their role. Though broadcasting now superseded the Press as the primary voice of government, the printed notice was by no means finished. On the contrary: while radio carried the general message, the detail (of which there was much) called for spelling out in black and white. In a seemingly endless stream, warnings, instructions, exhortations and, in some circumstances, threats [233] appeared. Scarcely an aspect of civilian life escaped attention.

For Authority, the value of the printed notice lay not only in its ability to deal with detail but in its relative durability; the chapter-and-verse of control – invisible, and even ignorable – over the radio, in print acquired an air of legal force and inescapability.

Armies and units of military government carried their notice-production units with them. Working initially from mobile presses and later from occupied printing works, they produced proclamations, regulations and controls to order.

In some cases (as with Louis-Napoleon, who pre-printed a proclamation with the date-line 'Boulogne' before setting out from London to liberate the town) notices were produced, undated, in advance. On other occasions they sprang from the central moment of invasion. In the German occupation of the Channel Islands in 1940, though production of notices and proclamations soon settled into a routine [229, 230, 231], the first put out by the invaders filled the whole of the front page of the island's newspapers. These, cleared of whatever news content had been planned for them, but still bearing their respective mastheads, served the dual role of news story and notice; they enumerated fourteen instructions to the population and were signed by the 'German Commandant of the Island of Jersey'. The notices were posted up all over the island.

On another invasion occasion some four years later there was clearer evidence of forward planning. An undated pre-printed notice appeared in English and German; it was headed 'Proclamation No 1' and was signed by Dwight D Eisenhower, Supreme Commander, Allied Expeditionary Force. It was posted up all over Northern France.

Department of survivals

Most of the notices discussed so far are now museum exhibits or items in collections of national or social history. But there is another sector, often more readily accessible, in which the public notice serves as indicator of the past. In inconspicuous public places, ignored by all except committed notice-watchers, neglected admonitions may keep their station into extreme old age. Some of them, particularly those in Britain, may outlive their relevance by many scores of years. Some are undoubted centenarians. This is understandable: while it is somebody's job to put them up, it is nobody's job to take them down. And often, like those that still protect the bridges in twentieth-century Dorset, their outrageous old age becomes a matter for the environmental conservationist.

Most of them survive by accident. All of them reflect attitudes and manners long since gone. The warning to loiterers at Wadebridge [151] still warns. In similar vein, and, at least until recently, present at a deserted beach at Lochinver: *Visitors are*
(page 123)

RAMSGATE.

AT a Meeting of the Inhabitants of the Town of Ramsgate, held purfuant to public notice, the 4th day of Auguft, 1803.

The DEPUTY in the Chair.

Refolved unanimoufly,

That a loyal, dutiful, and humble Addrefs be prefented to his Majefty, declaring our firm determination to fupport his Majefty and his government, by every exertion in our power, in carrying on the juft and necessary war, into which we are plunged by the infatiable ambition of our inveterate and unprincipled Enemy, who, almoft in our view, prefumes to threaten us by boafted preparations, with nothing lefs than our utter deftruction as a free and independent nation.

Refolved, That the following Addrefs be adopted, viz.

" *To the King's most excellent Majesty.*

" WE, your Majefty's dutiful and loyal fubjects, the Inhabitants of the town of Ramfgate, in the Town-hall affembled, approach your Majefty with the warmeft fentiments of attachment to our glorious and happy conftitution, enjoyed under your Majefty's mild and paternal government. The reftlefs and infatiable ambition of our inveterate and unprincipled enemy, who has forced us into the miferies of war, and who now arrogantly avows his determination to fubvert and overthrow our liberties, laws, and religion, and every thing dear to a free and independent nation, loudly and earneftly calls forth all claffes of your Majefty's faithful fubjects to unite with hand and heart in offering to your Majefty their ftrenuous and active exertions to defeat the defperate and vain boaftings of this haughty foe. With ardent alacrity we join our fellow fubjects on this important occafion, and with the utmoft cheerfulnefs offer to your Majefty our beft fervices, affured that your Majefty's goodnefs will reftore to us, whenever it can be obtained with honour and fecurity, the ineftimable bleffings of peace."

Refolved, that the Lord Warden of the Cinque Ports be requefted to prefent the above Addrefs to his Majefty. That the Deputy, the Rev. Mr. Harvey, and Mr. Gibfon, do perfonally attend the Lord Warden on the occafion.

Refolved, That the Deputation be defired to confer with the Lord Warden, on the beft mode of defence.

Refolved, That the Refolutions and Addrefs, be publifhed in a Canterbury, and a London Paper, and be printed and circulated through the town.—Adjourned.

P. Burgefs, Printer, Queen Street, Ramfgate.

207 Amiens 1918

208 New York 1917

209 Dorchester 1914

210 London 1915

211 Langemarck (Western Front) 1917

NOTICE

PROF. ALEXANDER

GENUINE HYPNOTIST, ELECTRICIAN AND BLOODLESS SURGEON.

Introducing MISS BERTHY BINGGALLI

The TRANCE MEDIUM, and the Famous ELECTROCUTION CHAIR, in which the Medium has passed through her body 150,000 Volts of Electricity without inflicting the Slightest injury. The Subject is also submitted for inspection to any member of the audience, and THE MOST MYSTERIOUS EFFECTS are produced by the Aid of Hypnotism, in which the Greatest Manifestations are obtained, the Clairvoyance and Somnambulism are remarkable and absolutely genuine and in this deep state of Hypnosis, Cures are Performed by me. Effects and Results of Hypnotism will always remain a profound Mystery, and in Genuine and Expert Hands good work is executed. Professor ALEXANDER is also at your service to TREAT CASES such as :—

SHELLSHOCK, PARALYSIS, SLEEP-WALKING, any Child who is Backward in Study, and BAD HABITS of any kind PERMANENTLY REMOVED, Etc.

Don't be afraid to offer yourself for Treatment, it will be FREE to you, and I also like to point out that I am not in discord with the Medical Gentlemen, as the Medical Profession cannot be done without, as there are certain cases which MUST require Medical Aid, and I can safely say that Doctors and Hypnotists of all Classes, Genuine, of course, always ought to work in Harmony and on friendly terms together.

Prof. ALEXANDER.

Moody Bros., Printers, Needless Alley, Birmingham.

212 Birmingham 1917

213 (?) Western Front 1916

215 Robecq (Western Front) 1918

216 Longueval (Western Front) 1916

Shooting on this Property is Prohibited

WAR

PROTECT THE BIRDS AS A WAR MEASURE!

The food destroyed in America by insects and small rodents would feed the people of Belgium! Birds are the great natural enemies of these pests. The laws of this State and of the Nation protect insect-eating birds, but many are being shot wantonly and for food. Report violations to the nearest game warden or to the address given below.

PROTEGGETE GLI UCCELLI COME MISURA DI SICUREZZA PER LA GUERRA!

Il cibo distrutto in America dagl'insetti e dai piccoli animali rosicanti basterebbe per nutrire il popolo Belga! Gli uccelli sono i nemici naturali più accanniti di questa peste d'insetti. Le leggi di questo Stato e della Nazione proteggono gli uccelli insettivori, ma disgraziatamente molti vengono uccisi maliziosamente o per cibo. Notificate queste violazioni al guardia-caccia più vicino oppure all'indirizzo dato qui sotto.

National Association of Audubon Societies

1974 BROADWAY ::   ::   :: NEW YORK CITY

217 New York 1917

POLICE NOTICE
AS TO LIGHTS IN LONDON.

The Secretary of State for the Home Department, under the powers conferred on him by Regulation 11 of the Defence of the Realm (Consolidation) Regulations, 1914, has made an Order which contains the undermentioned provisions:—

In all brightly lighted streets and squares and on bridges a portion of the lights must be extinguished so as to break up all conspicuous groups or rows of lights: and the lights which are not so extinguished must be lowered or made invisible from above by shading them or by painting over the tops and upper portions of the globes: provided that while thick fog prevails the normal lighting of the streets may be resumed.

Sky signs, illuminated fascias, illuminated lettering and lights of all descriptions used for outside advertising or for the illumination of shop fronts must be extinguished.

The intensity of the inside lighting of shop fronts must be reduced from 6 p.m. or earlier if the Commissioner of Police on any occasion so directs.

In tall buildings which are illuminated at night the greater part of the windows must be shrouded, but lights of moderate brightness may be left uncovered at irregular intervals.

All large lighted roof areas must be covered over or the lighting intensity reduced to a minimum.

The lighting of railway stations, sidings and goods yards must be reduced to the intensity sufficient for the safe conduct of business there. The upper half of the globes of all arc lights must be shaded or painted over.

Lights along the water front must be masked to prevent as far as practicable the reflection of the light upon the water.

The lights of trams and omnibuses must not be more than is sufficient to enable fares to be collected, and must be obscured while crossing bridges.

The use of powerful lamps on motor and other vehicles is prohibited.

Every person who shall cause or permit any vehicle during the period between one hour after sunset and one hour before sunrise, to travel in any street, highway, or road, to which the public have access, shall provide such vehicle with a lamp or lamps in proper working order and so constructed and capable of being so attached as when lighted to display to the rear a red light visible for a reasonable distance; and every person driving or being in charge of any such vehicle during such period as aforesaid shall keep such lamp or lamps properly trimmed, lighted, and attached.

For the purpose of this Order, the word "vehicle" shall include any bicycle, tricycle or velocipede, and any vehicle drawn or propelled by hand.

The aggregation of flares in street markets or elsewhere is prohibited.

In case of a sudden emergency, all instructions given by the Admiralty or by the Commissioner of Police on the advice of the Admiralty as to the further reduction or extinction of lights shall be immediately obeyed.

This Order shall apply to the City of London and the whole of the Metropolitan Police District, and, except where otherwise provided, to the hours between sunset and sunrise, and it shall be in force until it is by a further Order revoked.

Metropolitan Police Office,
New Scotland Yard, S.W.,
14th December, 1914.

E. R. HENRY,
The Commissioner of Police of the Metropolis.

Printed by the Receiver for the Metropolitan Police District, New Scotland Yard S.W.

218
London
1914

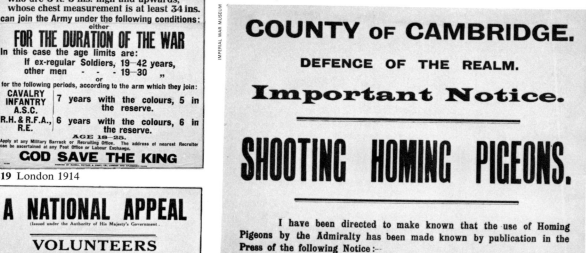

G. R.

FOR THOSE WHO WANT TO SERVE THEIR COUNTRY

Men who are medically fit,
who are 5 ft. 3 ins. high and upwards,
whose chest measurement is at least 34 ins.
can join the Army under the following conditions:

either

FOR THE DURATION OF THE WAR

In this case the age limits are:
If ex-regular Soldiers, 19—42 years,
other men - - - 19—30 ,,

or

for the following periods, according to the arm which they join:

| CAVALRY INFANTRY A.S.C. | 7 years with the colours, 5 in the reserve. |
| R.H. & R.F.A., R.E. | 6 years with the colours, 6 in the reserve. |

AGE 18—25.

Apply at any Military Barrack or Recruiting Office. The address of nearest Recruiter can be ascertained at any Post Office or Labour Exchange.

GOD SAVE THE KING

PRINTED BY ROBERL, HUNTER & SMITH, LTD., LONDON AND AYLESBURY—10274

219 London 1914

A NATIONAL APPEAL

(Issued under the Authority of His Majesty's Government.)

VOLUNTEERS
Urgently Required.

Men, Women, and Children must be Fed.
Essential Services must be maintained.

FOR THIS PURPOSE VOLUNTEERS
ARE URGENTLY NEEDED.

ARE YOU PREPARED TO SERVE?

If so, give in your name to-day!

You will be called upon in your turn.

EVERY KIND OF VOLUNTEER HELP WANTED.

Arrangements for Pay will be made
according to Duties Performed.

Register your name To-day at
The Local Volunteer Recruiting Office at the:—

ST. ANDREW'S HALL

PHILIP HENRIQUES,
Chairman of Volunteer Service Committee.

PRINTED BY "SURREY ADVERTISER," GUILDFORD.

221 Guildford 1926

THE WAR.
NOTICE.

Recipients of Relief from the National Relief Fund, or from any other source, are respectfully informed that they will not be served in this establishment with anything more than necessary refreshment.

Issued by the authority of the Wholesale and Retail Licensed Trade Associations in the Greater Birmingham Area, and to be PROMINENTLY displayed in the windows, and about Licensed Houses.

Extra copies will be supplied, gratis, on application to
Liverpool Chambers, Cherry Street, Birmingham, September 3rd, 1914.

220 Liverpool 1914

COUNTY OF CAMBRIDGE.

DEFENCE OF THE REALM.

Important Notice.

SHOOTING HOMING PIGEONS.

I have been directed to make known that the use of Homing Pigeons by the Admiralty has been made known by publication in the Press of the following Notice:—

"It has been decided to use Carrier Pigeons for certain purposes in connection with His Majesty's Service. The Public are therefore requested to refrain from shooting or otherwise interfering with Carrier Pigeons."

It occasionally happens, when bearing a message, birds may drop and be captured or killed. As there will be an ownership in pigeons used on His Majesty's Service, whoever appropriates them will be liable to a heavy penalty. If by chance any such exhausted or untrained "homer" carrying a message should be captured or come into possession of any person this should be notified to the Police, who will at once telegraph to the Admiralty copy of the message and the ring number, and by first post afterwards transmit the message itself to the Admiralty, London, and detain the bird until owned.

The pigeons to be used in this service will occasionally be sent to distant railway stations and liberated for exercising purposes.

CHARLES STRETTEN, M.V.O.,

County Constabulary Office,
Cambridge.
30th November, 1914.

Chief Constable of Cambridgeshire.

EXPRESS PRINTING WORKS, KING STREET, CAMBRIDGE.

222 Cambridge 1914

DO NOT STAND ABOUT HERE. EVEN IF YOU ARE NOT HIT SOMEONE ELSE WILL BE.

23 Western Front *c* 1915

O.M.S.

ORGANISATION FOR MAINTENANCE OF SUPPLIES.

Notice to ALL

Join the Organisation for Maintenance of Supplies.

Leatherhead and District Branch.

The O.M.S. is without Politics and of no Party.
The O.M.S. will in NO way interfere with Strikes or Lockouts of ANY description.

In the event of any disruption in this country which would stop the transport of vital necessities for the Community, the object of the O.M.S. will be to maintain supplies of Food, Fuel, etc., to each and all, and especially women and children who are the chief sufferers in all prolonged disputes.

THE O.M.S. IS GETTING THOUSANDS OF NEW MEMBERS EVERY WEEK.

**Each Citizen can help.
Every Citizen should join.**

Apply for further particulars to :-

NOTICE.

It should be made clear that men and women are recruited under this scheme in the interests of the Community and not for the purpose of acting as strike-breakers.

They are engaged with Government assistance solely to produce, handle or transport necessary food, fuel, light and power, or to perform such other duties as may from time to time be held by the Civil Commissioner to be essential in the various areas for the maintenance of the well-being of the Community.

All those engaging labour through the Volunteer Service Committee will be held responsible for seeing that this stipulation is adhered to, and any complaint of infringement of this agreement should be addressed to the Civil Commission of the Division, who will make such investigation and take such action as may be required.

PRINTED BY "SURREY ADVERTISER," GUILDFORD.

224 Leatherhead 1926   **225** Guildford 1926

113

The Royal Borough of Kensington.

NOTICE TO INHABITANTS.

Air-Raid Precautions

Issue of Respirators.

During the past few days a considerable number of ratepayers have enquired what arrangements would be made for issuing respirators in the event of a national emergency.

<u>Should it become necessary</u> to issue respirators, notice will be given by poster throughout the Borough. For some weeks there have been in store in bulk in Kensington sufficient respirators for the normal population. If a national emergency arises in the near future and it becomes necessary to issue respirators, arrangements will be made for them to be assembled and issued at the polling stations normally used at elections.

Personal enquiries should be made at the Air-Raid Precautions Offices at No. 92a, Kensington High Street or No. 134, Ladbroke Grove.

PLEASE SHOW THIS NOTICE TO ALL PERSONS RESIDING AT YOUR PREMISES.

F. WEBSTER,

Town Clerk.

Truscotts, London.

226 London 1938

FROM THE

EMERGENCY COMMITTEE,

UCKFIELD DISTRICT.

In the event of Invasion by Germany on the Southern Coast.

The Civil Population, not acting as Special Constables or in helping the Military, should be prepared to move, probably in a north westerly direction.

1. Each person should take with them food for two days and a blanket.

2. All main roads must be avoided, specially those to London.

3. Owners of spare Vehicles will be expected to assist in the removal of infirm persons and young children.

4. It is very important that the surnames of children should be sewn into their clothing, as in France and Belgium many small children who got separated from their parents have never been identified.

STOCK.

5. All Stock and Pigs not required by the Army must be removed or be destroyed, (by shooting or otherwise, but not with the knife.)

FORAGE.

Forage will probably have to be destroyed and all Vehicles not removed must be rendered useless.

It must clearly be understood that none of the above steps are to be taken except on the orders of the Military Authorities to be given by the Special Constables, and that no compensation can be claimed for anything destroyed, otherwise than by such orders.

R. J. STREATFEILD,

Chairman.

Harcourt Smith, Printer, Uckfield.

227 Uckfield 1940

228 Covent Garden *c* 1941 [1969]

114

Orders of the Commandant of the German Forces in Occupation of the Bailiwick of Jersey.

Dated the 8th day of July, 1940

1. The German Commandant is in close touch with the Civil Authorities and acknowledge their loyal co-operation.

2. The Civil Government and Courts of the Island will continue to function as heretofore, save that all Laws, Ordinances, Regulations and Orders will be submitted to the German Commandant before being enacted.

3. Such legislation as, in the past, required the Sanction of His Britannic Majesty in Council for its validity, shall henceforth be valid on being approved by the German Commandant and thereafter sanctioned by the Bailiff of Jersey.

4. The orders of the German Commandant heretofore, now and hereafter issued shall, in due course, be Registered in the Records of the Island of Jersey, in order that no person may plead ignorance thereof. Offences against the same, saving those punishable under German Military Law, shall be punishable by the Civil Courts, who shall enact suitable penalties in respect of such offences, with the approval of the German Commandant.

5. Assemblies in Churches and Chapels for the purpose of Divine Worship are permitted. Prayers for the British Royal Family and for the welfare of the British Empire may be said. Church Bells may ring ten minutes before Service. Such Assemblies shall not be made the medium for any propaganda or utterances against the honour or interests of, or offensive to the German Government or Forces.

6. Cinemas, Concerts and other Entertainments are permitted, subject to the conditions set out in Order No. 5 above.

7. Prices must not be increased or decreased. Any shopkeeper offending against this Order is liable to have his shop closed and also to pay any fine that may be imposed by the Competent Authorities.

8. The sale and consumption of wines, beer and cider is permitted in such premises as are licensed by the Civil Authorities.

9. Holders of Licences for the sale of such intoxicating liquors (wines, beer or cider), shall take the most rigid precautions for the prevention of drunkenness. If drunkenness takes place on such licensed premises, then without prejudice to any other civil penalty, the Island Police shall and are hereby empowered to close the premises.

10. All traffic between Jersey and Guernsey is prohibited, whether direct or indirect, for the time being (other Regulations will follow).

11. The Rate of Exchange between the Reichsmark and the Pound has been fixed at eight marks to the pound.

12. The continuance of the privileges granted to the civilian population is dependent upon their good behaviour. Military necessity, however, may, from time to time, require the Orders now in force to be made more stringent.

For and on behalf of the German Commandant of the Channel Islands

(Signed) GUSSEK, Hauptmann,

Commandant, Jersey.

PROCLAMATION

1.
It is forbidden to circulate enemy propaganda material by hand, or to spread the contents thereof.

2.
All enemy propaganda material found must be handed in immediately to the Feld Kommandantur, Victoria College Boarding House.

3.
Enemy propaganda material in the sense of this proclamation includes all publications which have not been issued or expressly authorized by the German administration department.

4.
In so far as no other penal-law imposes a heavy sentence, contraventions of this proclamation shall be punished according to paragraph 4 of the Special Military Criminal-Law of the 17th August, 1938, with a term of imprisonment not exceeding 15 years. In particularly mild cases a fine may be imposed.

Chief of the Military Administration Department for the Nord-West of France.

July 29th, 1940.

230 Jersey 1940

PROCLAMATION

Certain incidents have occurred in which, on the part of the inhabitants of the Island, acts have been committed which were against the safety of the Army of Occupation. Those who were guilty have been, or will be, punished according to the decree of Martial Law by Sentence of Death.

In their own interest I warn the Public most solemnly against perpetrating any further acts of this kind. Any person involved in such an act, either as Perpetrator, Participant or Instigator will, upon conviction by Court Martial, without power of Appeal be condemned to suffer the Death Penalty.

In view of the present economic situation the recent Prohibition in regard to Fishing has been modified. If, however, this act of leniency is misunderstood, and certain individual and irresponsible elements of the population perpetrate further acts which are detrimental to the safety of the Army of Occupation, the entire population will have to suffer the consequences of the reprisals which will follow.

People of the Island! Your destiny and your welfare is in your own hands. Your Home Interests demand that you should refrain from, and to the best of your power prevent, all such actions which must inevitably be followed by such disastrous consequences.

The Military Commander in France,
(Signed) v. STÜLPNAGEL,
General of Infantry.

231 Jersey c 1941

232 Jersey 1941

ATTENTION—WARNING

Any persons found marking walls with 'V' signs or insults against the German Armed Forces are liable to be shot.

A reward will be paid to any persons giving information that will lead to the arrest of these offenders.

G. V. Schmettow

General,
German Military Government

233 Jersey 1941

REWARD

A REWARD WILL BE GIVEN to any person giving information about anyone who marks on any visible place the letter V or any other words or signs calculated to offend the German Authorities Eighth day of July **1941**

KOMMANDANTUR 515
Schumacher KOMMANDANT

234 Jersey 1941

MILITARY GOVERNMENT—GERMANY
SUPREME COMMANDER'S AREA OF CONTROL
PROCLAMATION No. I

TO THE PEOPLE OF GERMANY:

I, General Dwight D. Eisenhower, Supreme Commander, Allied Expeditionary Force, do hereby proclaim as follows:—

I.

The Allied Forces serving under my command have now entered Germany. We come as conquerors, but not as oppressors. In the area of Germany occupied by the forces under my command, we shall obliterate Nazi-ism and German Militarism. We shall overthrow the Nazi rule, dissolve the Nazi Party and abolish the cruel, oppressive and discriminatory laws and institutions which the Party has created. We shall eradicate that German Militarism which has so often disrupted the peace of the world. Military and Party leaders, the Gestapo and others suspected of crimes and atrocities will be tried and, if guilty, punished as they deserve.

II.

Supreme legislative, judicial and executive authority and powers within the occupied territory are vested in me as Supreme Commander of the Allied Forces and as Military Governor, and the Military Government is established to exercise these powers under my direction. All persons in the occupied territory will obey immediately and without question all the enactments and orders of the Military Government. Military Government Courts will be established for the punishment of offenders. Resistance to the Allied Forces will be ruthlessly stamped out. Other serious offences will be dealt with severely.

III.

All German courts and educational institutions within the occupied territory are suspended. The Volksgerichtshof, the Sondergerichte, the SS Police Courts and other special courts are deprived of authority throughout the occupied territory. Re-opening of the criminal and civil courts and educational institutions will be authorized when conditions permit.

IV.

All officials are charged with the duty of remaining at their posts until further orders, and obeying and enforcing all orders or directions of Military Government or the Allied Authorities addressed to the German Government or the German people. This applies also to officials, employees and workers of all public undertakings and utilities and to all other persons engaged in essential work.

DWIGHT D. EISENHOWER,
General,
Supreme Commander,
Allied Expeditionary Force.

MILITÄRREGIERUNG—DEUTSCHLAND
KONTROLLGEBIET DES OBERSTEN BEFEHLSHABERS
PROKLAMATION Nr. I

AN DAS DEUTSCHE VOLK:

Ich, General Dwight D. Eisenhower, Oberster Befehlshaber der Alliierten Streitkräfte gebe hiermit Folgendes bekannt:

235
Germany
1944

117

237 New York 1972

236 New York 1972

239 Reading 1969

238 Wimborne *c* 1925 [1969]

240 Mount Kenya 1969

41 New York 1972

PETER SCOTT

242 Donegal 1957

244 Dorset 1970

245 Purbeck House, Swanage 1876 [1969]

Young GIRLS WANTED FOR PICKLING & BOTTLING. ☞ **APPLY WITHIN.**

246 (?) *c* 1900

GENTLEMEN CYCLISTS PLEASE DISMOUNT

247

THIS WALL IS THE ENTIRE PROPERTY OF THE COUNTY OF MIDDLESEX.

248 Islington *c* 1835 [1972]

NO CAMPING. **NOTICE** BY ORDER. ANIMALS GRAZING IN THIS COMMON WITHOUT A LICENCE WILL BE IMPOUNDED BY THE HAYWARDS.
BY ORDER
AGENTS FOR THE

249 Corfe Castle *c* 1950 [1970]

Manly WOMEN'S BOWLING CLUB

250 Manly, Sydney 1970

FORT SCAUR WELCOMES VISITORS. NO ADMISSION. TOILET FACILITIES AVAILABLE.

251 Fort Scaur *c* 1970

STANDING IN WASH BASINS IS STRICTLY PROHIBITED

252 Metropolitan Music Hall, London; (Dressing room) *c* 1950

CAB RANK FOR 1 CAB

253 London 1971

End

254 London 1970

NO VEHICLE TO REVERSE INTO STREET

255 London 1970

City of Westminster. HORSE & DOLPHIN YARD
LOW CEILING HEIGHT 7'0'6"
NO LORRIES OVER THIS HEIGHT ALLOWED

256 London 1971

SLOW THROUGH ARCH PLEASE! TURKEYS & TWINS

257 Garinish 1956

MOTOR CYCLES MAY NOT BE RIDDEN INSIDE COLLEGE

258 London University 1970

DRIVERS OF VEHICLES ARE REQUESTED TO KEEP TO THE RECOGNISED ROAD

259 Corfe Castle *c* 1950 [1969]

260 Sydney 1970

261 Swanage 1970

262 Dorset *c* 1855 [*c* 1968]

263 London 1970

Store detectives operating

WARNING

THE CONSUMPTION OF ALCOHOL AND DRUG TAKING IN PUBLIC
N SPACES HAS LED TO SERIOUS ACTS OF MISCONDUCT AND
PLAINTS OF NUISANCE FROM THE PUBLIC.
THE ATTENDANT ON DUTY WILL CALL THE POLICE
EDIATELY ANY BREACH OF THE CORPORATION'S BYELAWS
URS.

ANUARY 1968   CITY ENGINEER

265 London 1968

NOTICE

If any building plant or materials
are being removed from this site
on Saturdays and Sundays
or between 5 p.m. and 8 a.m. on
other days they are being <u>stolen.</u>
Please note the number of any
vehicle being used and then
immediately telephone the police.

266 London 1969

HOPLIFTERS WILL
BE PROSECUTED
NOT WARNED

267 London 1970

---

earnestly requested to refrain from profaning the Sabbath day by indulging in any form of recreation. Among surviving bygones, concern for seemly behaviour is widespread. The Market House at Ledbury carries a caution from the local magistrates (December 1872) warning that *persons creating a noise or disturbance in or near the public street are guilty of a MISDEMEANOUR and are liable to FINE AND IMPRISONMENT.*

The battle for seemliness

The presence of street traders, itinerants and others was also viewed as unseemly. The instruction to the porter at Staple Inn, London (also still surviving [150]) is explicit. So is a similar injunction at Newton-le-Willows, where nuisances include 'hawkers, traders and ballad-singers'. Rude boys were a perennial pest (as both Staple Inn and Hythe [145] testify), and the matter of 'nuisances' was no less tiresome: one surviving nuisance notice is reported as saying, *Commit no Nuisance in this Alley: Beware of the Bye-Law.*

Notices about spitting survive, for the most part, only in museums [147, 148]. Many of them are strangely wordy; Renfrew is reported to have had, until recent times, at least one such; it said *Please do not Expectorate on the Pavement.* On the whole, however, the tone of survivals is distinctly harsh; a faded anti-billposting specimen on a church wall at Edinburgh reads *Stick no Bills Here: Offenders will be Punished.* The style of lettering proclaims this last as dating from around the 1830s, when notices of prohibition were markedly outspoken and punishments severe. (This was the era of the man-trap and spring gun; one estate in the West Country carried a sign saying simply *Take Notice that all Persons found Trespassing in this Orchard will be Shot.*)

The matter of punishment has undoubtedly eased. Set against the rigours of shooting, transportation, penal servitude for life, flogging and so forth, twentieth-century threats appear distinctly moderate. Perhaps no prohibitory notice has ever achieved the degree of restraint shown by the present-day Cranborne Parish Council. Spelling out its name as a title-piece, it expresses itself in the cast-iron idiom of the Dorset bridge notices: *NO LITTER PLEASE. Depositing of litter is liable to police action and a fine under Government bye-laws. The above Council hope that such action will not be required.*

Among British bygones only recently disappeared, a significant number relate to behaviour between the sexes. The Borough of Margate declared (initially in 1862) that 'a distance of not less than sixty feet shall be preserved by the Owners or Drivers of Bathing Machines from which Females are bathing and those from which Males are bathing'. And that no person was to bathe within a hundred yards 'without wearing drawers or a gown or a dress or other such suitable covering as will prevent any indecent exposure of the person', and that 'persons found bathing . . . without drawers . . . may be arrested and detained by a Constable'.

A notice on Plymouth Hoe, similarly concerned, said GENTLEMEN ARE REQUESTED NOT TO OVERLOOK THE LADIES' BATHING PLACE. In converse sense, a stretch of the river bank at Oxford, much used by gentlemen swimmers, carried the warning NO LADIES BEYOND THIS POINT. Ladies, on the whole, were a difficulty. Until just before World War II a summer-house notice survived in Dorset Square, London, saying *Gentlemen are Requested not to Smoke in the Garden while Ladies are Present.*

Another major preoccupation was the horse. Among survivals, cabs, cabmen, horsemen and horses still linger. The warning to cabmen about skylarking [146] is now in a museum; so is a canal-side notice saying that 'Any captain riding his horse . . . will be dismissed from the company's service' And the cryptic HORSES HEADS EAST (a turn-of-the-century parking instruction to hackney carriages on the Embankment) has disappeared. But *Drivers Please Dismount and Lead Horse Through Arch* (Cheyne Walk) has survived. And *Drive Slowly; Motors Sound Horn* was still visible at Euston in 1971.

Some half-a-dozen surviving notices instructing drivers to 'Slacken Bearing Rein' disappeared only in the late sixties, and two others threatened prosecution to drivers who damaged the road by 'descending the hill with a locked wheel which has not a properly adjusted skid-pan'. (Another threatened proceedings against drivers damaging the road with the skid-pan . . .)

Most evocative of all horse-era notices is the one still to be seen in the entrance-way to the Phoenix Hotel in Dorchester. It says *Bicycles Etc. are NOT to be left in this Passage. They are to be left in charge of the Ostler. No responsibility will be accepted for any Horses Etc. putting up at this Establishment.*

Until their nationalization in 1948, Britain's railways were a fertile field for survivals; some of the items now in the Museum of British Transport were still at work in the early 1950s. Passengers using the station at Lime Street Liverpool recall with affection the legend *This Lift is for the Use of Porters with Carriage Lamps and Footwarmers.* Bridges, too, offered a fair yield. In addition to their sensitivity on the score of wilful damage they were often uncertain as to their own capacities. The 'Great Weight' item [262] is typical; others, also still in place, warn of dangers of attempting to cross in 'Locomotives and other Ponderous Vehicles'.

Open-space survivors include the park-seat protector at Islington Green, London [149], and the sentinel at the entrance to Christ Church Meadow, Oxford [144], still on duty at this writing, and still envisaging its dire miscellany of persons carrying parcels, wheeling barrows, flying kites, throwing stones, bowling, hooping, firing guns and pistols, birdnesting, and cutting names on seats.

Among survival grounds in less public places, schools, hospitals and other institutions are likely locations. Examples may remain in the recollection of inmates for generations. At Harrow School in the 1920s each lavatory bore the advice: *One steady pull will cause the flushing cistern to discharge its contents: do not jerk the chain or hold the same down once the flush has commenced.* The form of words was engraved upon pupils' memories. 'One steady pull' became a by-word; an old Harrovian recalls that he was greeted on a dark night in the Western Desert in World War II with the words, 'One steady pull will help a lot here . . .'

Motor-cars and oddities

The twentieth-century notice is dominated, like most other aspects of our time, by the motor car. Sydney's motorway message to errant one-way drivers (*Go back; you are going the wrong way* [260]) conveys a deeper truth than may appear.

Since its first emergence the car has generated multitudes of notices – initially temperate but, with the passage of time, increasingly brusque. One survival in Central London, dating from well before World War II, if not from before World War I, is already mildly petulant: THIS STREET, it says, IS TOO NARROW FOR LARGE MOTORS TO PASS THROUGH. The notice of the seventies is less inclined to reason with the reader; the one-word injunction behind a quiet London hotel [263] is typical.

In some areas the notice-maker has tired of the normal imperatives. In Marine, Illinois, a notice reads: WELCOME TO MARINE. NO RADAR CONTROL. NO ELECTRIC TIMING. DRIVE CAREFULLY. From the Isle of

Wight come reports of another gambit – this time throwing the onus of his safety directly upon the driver: *Motorists are warned to get out of their car and inspect the road before proceeding.* (If the syntax is doubtful, deceleration-value is not.) Other notices calculated to intrigue rather than to command, are Alaska's *Caution: Dog Team Crossing* and Kenya's *Slow down: Equator*.

Animals are another rewarding field. The interface of animal and motorcar provides much notice-matter: the car-park of at least one Canadian hotel carries an intimation to the effect that the management will not be responsible for damage done to parked cars by bears. In Kenya, roadside reminders point out that *Elephants Have Right of Way*.

Elsewhere there are strong suggestions of animal literacy. New York's pavement hint [237] is one. Another is the request to elephants at a bridge on Mount Kenya [240]. Another, again in New York, appears in a local post office; it says *No Dogs Allowed* – but an afterthought below says *Except Seeing-Eye Dogs*. Animals at Corfe Castle [249] require not only literacy, but a licence.

Pitfalls in the wording of the public notice abound. The heading IMBECILE WARD KEEPERS [56] and the County of Middlesex's property declaration [248] provide awful warnings. So does the call for Young Girls for Pickling and Bottling [246]. The twentieth century, with its improved notice-making facilities greatly multiplies the number of traps for the unwary. *Do not fail to miss our Air Display*, says an enthusiast in Queensland. *This Monument is in charge of Down County Council*, says Down County Council.

Other ambiguities include *We dispense with accuracy* (chemist, Lowestoft); *Ears pierced while you wait* (jeweller, London); *St Swithun's School for Girls Preparatory for Boys* (Winchester); *Stones are not allowed to be thrown into the water* (Windermere); *We will despatch your order to all parts of the world* (coffee shop, Soho); *These books are for sale, not for reading* (Croydon bookshop) and a bold-print instruction panel on a dismountable packing case: COLLAPSE AND RETURN TO BEDFORD.

In the matter of oddities, one report mentions a bricked-up passage-way, observed in London in 1937; a notice says *This Passage was temporarily Closed to the Public in 1789.* A coastal inlet in Kerry claims a notice saying *If two vessels should meet in this channel, both must stop and neither may proceed until the other one has passed.*

A further field includes juxtapositions, as in the request to cyclists [247]; incomprehensibles, such as the monosyllabic traffic sign at London's Hyde Park Corner [254]; the strange inversion at St Giles Court, Holborn [255] and Fort Scaur's curious contradiction [251]. London's CAB RANK FOR 1 CAB [253] falls into a category of its own; its logic has remained unchallenged for upwards of fifty years. Wimborne's SAFETY FIRST: DO NOT STAND ON BRIDGE [238] proves to be concerned not with the bridge's strength, but its narrowness.

No less diverting are the oddities of notices in foreign-language English. Some, it is to be feared, are apocryphal (*We are the Little Sisters of Mercy; we harbour all sorts of diseases, and no notice is taken of religion.*) But many are genuine. Reported from a Swiss hotel: *It is defended to circulate the corridors in the boots of ascension.* From Chamonix: *Take Care of the Glacier* and *The Dog is Wicked.* From a bar in Malaysia: *Ladies are not allowed in the Bar without husband, escort or similar.*

Occasionally the oddity is conscious: in the grounds of Frank Sinatra's estate a notice reads: *Anyone coming beyond this point better have a good reason.* In another such case a board says *Do not use this gate unless the dog knows you.* Sometimes oddity is merely quirky: in a Bloomsbury hotel a fifth floor telephone notice is reported as saying *To call the operator, shout downstairs.*

It would be wrong, however, to conclude that the public notice of today is all motorcar and oddity. Though often much briefer than its forebears, its tone is in general no less sharp, its subject matter often no less grim. Crime continues lively [38, 40, 236, 261, 264, 267]; so does unseemly behaviour [39, 261, 265]. Grimmer altogether are notices that reflect the tensions of our time; in South Africa: SAFETY FIRST; CROSS BY THE SUBWAY; WHITES ONLY. In Ulster, outside an internment camp: KEEP OUT; SURVIVORS WILL BE PROSECUTED.

On the whole, though details change, general principles endure. *Store Detectives Operating* [264] is *Gentlemen, Tread Light* [85] in modern dress. Private property still appears to be firmly with us as an institution (as the picture on page 6 confirms); so are epidemics, shop assistants, warfare, unrest, prisons, bank robbers and tippling in public houses on Sundays. On present showing it is unlikely that by the 2070s many of these will have dropped out. And it is to be hoped that the collecting and collating of specimens will not stop here; the years ahead should yield some notable addenda.

ACKNOWLEDGEMENTS

The author and publishers acknowledge with thanks the help and advice of the following organizations:

Barrow-in-Furness Museum; Bodleian Library; British Post Office; Chartered Insurance Institute; Chubb & Son's Lock and Safe Company; Dorset County Museum; Dorset Military Museum; Guildhall Library; Inner London Education Authority; London Museum; London Transport; Marylebone Public Library; Metropolitan Police; Milton Abbas Museum; Museums Association; Museum of British Transport; Museum of English Rural Life; National Library of Ireland; National Union of Railwaymen; National Westminster Bank; Newark-on-Trent Museum; New York Public Library; New Zealand House Library; North Thames Gas Board; Norwich Union; Pitt Rivers Museum; St Bride Printing Library; St George in the East; Salisbury Museum; Scotland Yard; Sussex Constabulary; Trades Union Congress Library; Tower Hamlets Libraries Committee; Ulster Folk Museum; United States Information Service; Victoria and Albert Museum; Victory Poster Club; Wilberforce Museum.

Thanks are also due to the following individuals for their kindness in offering items for inclusion in the book:

Mrs E Anderson; R B Appleton Esq; A N A Argent Esq; T G L Ashwell Esq; W R Battersby Esq; A S Bell Esq; Pelham Bird Esq; F C B Black Esq; O J R de Boer Esq; Miss M E Bolt; E K Brownrigg Esq; F E Bruce Esq; Anthony Bushell Esq; Brian Burrough Esq; Jules Cave Esq; P R Catcheside Esq; B T Clackson Esq; Frank Collin Esq; Sir James Corry; E H Dodimead Esq; G Donaldson Esq; Garnett Don-Fox Esq; Mrs Kathleen Donovan; Barry Duncan Esq; F A Ellis Esq; Miss Irene Ellis; John Farrell Esq; Mrs J Feisenberger; William Fenton Esq; Mrs D Fetherstonhaugh; Mrs M Fitzherbert-Brockholes; Col Peter Fleming; Mrs J A Flute; Ian Forsyth Esq.; Mrs Gabrielle Foster; Mrs A M Freeman; P W Gaddum Esq; Mrs G Gammage; Miss Geraldine V Garnier; Peter Gathercole Esq; R M Gordon Esq; C E Goshawk Esq; Mrs Margaret Greer; Mrs Dorothy Griffin; P E Gutteridge Esq; Allan Hare Esq; Raymond Harris Esq; Mrs Johanna Harrison; Miss Renee Haynes; Miss Joyce E Hayward; Guy E G Hereward Esq; Martin Hills Esq; Geoffrey Holland Esq; Dr R P Holmes; Robert W Hopkinson Esq; R P Hurn Esq; Ralph Hyde Esq; G Jenkins Esq; F S Jennings Esq; Robert Kelly Esq; Peter Laws Esq; Christopher Lee Esq; Mrs S M Lloyd-Thomas; Charles Lulham Esq; Philip J Lund Esq; Bernard Malone Esq; Miss H Mason; D G Moore Esq; Mrs P E Moore; Mrs Katherine Newell; Mrs Mavis Nuttall; Colin Osman Esq; J Vernon Payne Esq; Mrs Rachel Pevison-Webber; G H L Plymen Esq; M A R Powers Esq; Miss Prudence Raper; C Rawlinson Esq; Lord Rea of Eskdale; H M Reynolds Esq; Harold Rickards Esq; Sir Sidney Ridley; Alan H Rigg Esq; Mrs L M Roberts; R G Robinson Esq; Edward B Scott Esq; Peter Scott Esq; Mrs Louise C Snell; J W Stead Esq; Charles Stiles Esq; M C Strover Esq; Miss Dorothy Stucky; Major A E Sturdy; Peter Tatlow Esq; Martin H Taylor Esq; Miss A Todd; Rupert Townshend-Rose Esq; Trevor L J Tritton Esq; Miss Catherine M Vincent; Mrs J Howard Wall; Mrs Mavis Walledge; H J Welch Esq; Miss M C Welsh; Peter West Esq; Alastair White Esq; Mrs Edith Williams; J P Wood Esq; Miss Margaret Woods; Mrs P T Woods; Herbert S Wright Esq; John Wymer Esq; W M Yool Esq.

INDEX

(Numerals in italics indicate illustration numbers, not pages)